THE OPAQUENESS OF GOD

BOOKS BY DAVID O. WOODYARD
PUBLISHED BY THE WESTMINSTER PRESS
The Opaqueness of God
To Be Human Now
Living Without God—Before God

THE OPAQUENESS
OF GOD

by DAVID O. WOODYARD

THE WESTMINSTER PRESS
Philadelphia

ISBN 0–664–20896–7

LIBRARY OF CONGRESS CATALOG CARD No. 78–117645

75–4048

PUBLISHED BY THE WESTMINSTER PRESS®
PHILADELPHIA, PENNSYLVANIA

PRINTED IN THE UNITED STATES OF AMERICA

CONTENTS

FOREWORD

EVEN THE MORE CASUAL READER in theology is aware that
the question of God has moved to the center. The evidence of this is indeed reassuring. But at the same time
it is disquieting that many of the trusted landmarks are
weathering. Those persons confident that their familiarity
with theologians like Karl Barth, Rudolf Bultmann, and
Paul Tillich has kept them in touch are shaken periodi-
cally by the new names crowding the scene. While a
person may feel he has played the game before, he is apt
to be overwhelmed by the presence of new players and
tactics with which he is unfamiliar. Given as many theologians are to writing lengthy and ponderous tomes, even
the trained despair of keeping up. This book attempts to
suggest the contours the question of God is taking as we
enter a new decade. Its objective is limited to introducing the reader to the literature available in English and
reporting some critical responses to the men studied.

As a title THE OPAQUENESS OF GOD is not intended so
much to suggest a theme as to make visible an assumption. One of the meanings of the word "opaque" is that
an object resists rays of light; that is, one cannot see into

it clearly. I find opaqueness a rather apt image to associate with God. By his very nature, he cannot be "seen
through" or "seen into." Finite man cannot grasp the
reality of God; the God who is really God cannot be fully
known. But this does not prevent man from taking sight
in a wide variety of ways; indeed the very opaqueness of
God stimulates and requires it. One of the most significant evidences of health in the contemporary theological
scene is the vitality and imagination that have produced
quite diverse approaches to the question of God. This
suggests that theologians are struggling with the reality
of God and not some penultimate phenomenon.

It may help the reader if we suggest briefly some data
about the men studied and indicate a starting point for
reading in primary sources.

Karl Barth (1886–1968) began his work in a Swiss parish
from which in 1918 he wrote *The Epistle to the Romans*,
which "fell like a bomb on the playground of the theologians." From this initial impact he was called to university posts at Göttingen, Münster, and then Bonn. By 1935
his refusal to cooperate with the Nazis necessitated leaving Bonn for Switzerland, where he became Professor of
Theology at Basel. He retired formally in 1962 but con-
tinued his sessions with students and received those who
came to Basel to engage one of the century's greatest
theologians. Barth is best understood through his massive
Church Dogmatics, but those not prepared to read some
ten thousand or more pages can benefit from Herbert
Hartwell's excellent study *The Theology of Karl Barth:
An Introduction*. For a brief exposure to Barth's writing
The Humanity of God is a good point of departure.

Rudolf Bultmann (b. 1884) distinguished himself as a New Testament scholar and theologian during his tenure at the University of Marburg from 1921 to 1951. He was Professor of New Testament Studies. His work is most frequently identified with the project of "demythologizing," which was his attempt to liberate the Biblical message from the thought patterns of another era. The more substantial breadth of his contribution is reflected in *Essays: Philosophical and Theological* and *Theology of the New Testament,* Volumes I and II. The general reader will benefit from reading *Jesus Christ and Mythology* plus several chapters in *Essays.*

Dietrich Bonhoeffer (1906–1945) was graduated from the University of Berlin and after a year in the parish at Barcelona returned as a Lecturer in Systematic Theology. He publicly denounced Hitler in 1933 and two years later was banned from Berlin. When the war formally broke out, he left the security of the United States and returned to Germany to work through the Confessing Church and mobilize opposition to Hitler. He was arrested by the Nazis in 1943 and hanged in 1945. His *Letters and Papers from Prison* certainly ranks as one of the most influential books during the last quarter century. Many readers find that *Life Together* and *The Cost of Discipleship* have had a comparable impact upon them.

Paul M. van Buren (b. 1924) earned his doctorate under Karl Barth at Basel. The influence of his mentor dominated his early years, but with the publication of *The Secular Meaning of the Gospel* in 1963 there was evidence of a clean break. Van Buren soon became identified in the eyes of the general public with the "death

of God" movement. This was both understandable and
unfortunate. Van Buren writes of a language and cultural
event and not something that happened to God. He is
currently Professor of Religion at Temple University. His
Secular Meaning of the Gospel is a readable book, but
those who want a more recent and succinct treatment
can read Chapters 2 and 8 in *Theological Explorations*.

Schubert M. Ogden (b. 1928) has quickly become one
of the most influential younger theologians on the American scene. In 1969 he returned as Professor of Theology
to the University of Chicago Divinity School from which
he had received his Ph.D. Ogden is of special interest
since he has drawn together an early interest in Bultmann
and existentialism with a formidable influence from
Alfred North Whitehead and process philosophy. This
combination has enabled him to speak forcefully both in
the realm of immediate experience and in a thought pat-
tern congenial with the sciences. The first chapter in *The
Reality of God* is difficult reading but an indispensable
introduction to his thought.

Fritz Buri (b. 1907) is one of the more exciting theologians in Europe, yet he remains relatively unknown in
America. He has combined a distinguished teaching and
writing career as Professor of Dogmatics in the University of Basel with a substantial ministry through the
Cathedral of Basel. Although remaining under the influence of Bultmann, he is one of his severest critics. An
early critic of the traditionalism in Barth, Bultmann, and
others of the neo-orthodox movement, he has turned in
his later years to the task of interpreting tradition. Some
of his most recent thought is available in a volume that

contains lectures given in this country under the title
How Can We Still Speak Responsibly of God?

Wolfhart Pannenberg (b. 1928) came under the influence
of Karl Barth twenty years ago when he studied at Basel,
and even in developing a polemic against his mentor,
continues to reflect some of that early schooling. The
Professor of Systematic Theology at the University of
Munich broke most decisively with Barth in the contention that theology must establish its case from public
evidence as it is subject to reason. Pannenberg argues for
faith from the facticity of history in a way most theologians had not thought possible a decade ago. While his
massive work on Christology, *Jesus—God and Man,* is his
most important work in English, an excellent introduction
to his thinking is available in *Theology and the Kingdom
of God.*

Jürgen Moltmann (b. 1926) is Professor of Systematic
Theology at the University of Tübingen. He has been
identified with a corps of theologians who are attempting
to interpret the Christian faith with hope as a central
theme. Believing that Christianity is forward-looking and
that this is the spirit of the time, he has developed an
understanding of futurity, which is at once intense and
compelling to a younger generation of theological students. Not fearing to work with the category of revolution, Moltmann has developed a following that may well
be a vanguard in both the church and the social order.
For a more systematic treatment, *The Theology of Hope*
is indispensable reading, but several chapters in *Religion,
Revolution, and the Future* would be a significant introduction.

It is more than his training and study that a man brings
with him to a book on the question of God. Even when
his contribution is not original but interprets the work
of others, his own being as a person is involved. That
being and the questions it raises has been formed by his
lived experience with significant others, most notably
his family. I can only confess that the love I have known,
first in the home of my birth and then in the home of my
marriage, has done more than anything to support my
confidence in the reality of God.

My colleague in the Religion Department at Denison
University, David A. Gibbons, has provided invaluable
guidance in the revision of this manuscript. My debts to
him in this project and in our common work are many.
Mrs. Barbara Philipps has suffered through the typing of
several drafts of this book without complaint and always
with a gracious spirit.

I dedicate this book to Roger Hazelton, judicious
theologian and gracious gentleman.

                                        D. O. W.

Denison University
Granville, Ohio

INTRODUCTION
The New Search
for the Meaning of God

AFTER LISTENING TO WILLIAM HAMILTON, exponent of the death of God, a college senior responded perceptively and surely on behalf of more than his own generation: "*Intellectually* his position does not intrigue me. If I were seeking a posture from which to be done with God, I would choose Jean-Paul Sartre's. But Hamilton does expose what I *feel*. When I attempt to speak of God, there is no lived experience which I can readily tap and release meaning and intensity into the word." Both the professional theologian and the laymen have the feeling that something has come between them and the language of transcendence. There can be scant comfort in public opinion polls that continue to indicate that over 90 percent of the American people still believe in God. It would not be audacious to suggest that the majority of those who answer affirmatively cannot go on and explain why, how, or what they mean by God. It is significant that the perennial bull sessions in college dormitories seldom focus on the issue of God; a decade ago it was at or near the top of the agenda. The degree to which God is a dead issue must be taken with considerable seriousness.

Yet among theologians the question of God has not
for years been so vital and intense as it is today. Their
concentration on the matter of God borders on an obses-
sion. What is distinctive about their task now is that to
some degree they have to create the issue as well as construct a response to it. They operate in an environment
that neither poses nor supports the question of God.
Theologians cannot even bounce off stalwart opponents.
In America the argument with atheists simply does not
persist with any substantial intensity. When one's opposition begins to evaporate, that reveals both the depth
of the problem and the complexity of constituting a
position.

It is becoming increasingly evident that the apparently
short-lived and sensational "death of God" movement has
had a lasting effect in that it has driven the discipline
of theology to seek new beginnings. These alleged radi-
cals not only identified something lost in our experience
but forced the professional community to attend in new
ways to the task of speaking of God. One younger theologian acknowledges this impact when he writes: "Their
questions are always in my mind. Their answers are
always challenging those I prefer. I share with them
some of the shock at witnessing the collapse of going
systems. Whether one cut his theological eyeteeth more
on Barth, Bultmann, or Tillich, the feeling is quite general that we can hardly go on the way we have been
going."[1] Increasingly a second generation of theologians
is experiencing the need to begin again and do theology
from a base beneath that on which their intellectual
fathers in the faith stood with confidence. It is no longer
possible to assume that we are with the question of God
or that the question of God is with us.

Those who in the past had been identified somewhat loosely and often incongruously with the title neo-orthodoxy operated with a confidence that the reality of God was not in question except for those who worked against it; and even that was a negative witness to faith on their terms. For the Barths, Bultmanns, and Tillichs, as well as a host of others, the meaningfulness of what they were doing was not in question. They could assume what is no longer possible to assume for those who take up the constructive task of theology in their wake. Younger theologians cannot be content with refining the positions and processes of their mentors; it is not viable to begin where they began, for it is their very assumptions which have been brought most radically in question. The question that has to be faced is whether or not it is possible to speak intelligibly of God. The shift we have experienced perceptibly in the last five years is from finding more adequate and relevant means of expressing transcendence to questioning, whether transcendence is a category about which it is meaningful to speak at all.

Langdon Gilkey, professor of systematic theology at the University of Chicago Divinity School, contributes some considerable precision to identifying the problem by saying that the issue has shifted from that of "validity" to that of "meaning."[2] Though on the surface it might seem otherwise, the latter is a more radical and devastating question. When someone says, "I understand what you are saying but do not myself believe there is a God," our affirmation is denied but the possibility of theological discourse is not challenged. It is accepted by both parties that it is justifiable to talk about God even if one does not choose to interpret his experience of himself and his world with respect to an Ultimate. On the other hand, to say, "When you use the word 'God,' I do not know what you could mean," we are questioning a form of thought. To be challenged at this level questions the possibility of discourse. More than the adequacy or viability of our concepts is at stake; the precise mode in which we think and speak has become suspect. It is vastly more difficult to communicate when the possibility of understanding is at stake than when it is the possibility of agreeing. When a person refutes my position, I can at least stay with him; when he disputes the categories in which I am thinking, we cease to share common ground. It is in the latter state we are more apt to find ourselves now. And it is this which requires of theology a new beginning rather than building confidently upon foundations laid by those who have most recently dominated the territory.

There is nothing new about the demand that theology pertain to its time. The world as it is experienced and conceived in a given era constitutes the arena within which faith must always find expression and make contact. It is the fate and fascination of theology to move between its understanding of the Christian message and the particular forms in which men experience their lives at given times. It operates as much by mood as model; when either is violated it yields to impertinence or irrelevance. Formulation of the faith is the art of speaking from the matrix of the age and the ageless. Thus theology always has a world or secular realm in which it transacts its business. But the anatomy of our present situation is one in which our worldly existence puts us at a greater distance from the faith than it has been in recent years. Religion is never without its "cultured despisers," but now it appears to be present as an alien from another planet who has no points of contact. The reality of the world is often subversive in relation to faith; it appears in this time that our experience immunizes us against faith in God.

What is distinctive in our time is its unprecedented secular spirit. This can mean at least two things. The more modest claim would be that man neither intuitively nor reflectively is disposed to respond to his lived experience in the framework of a theistic affirmation. The question of God may persist as something of a cultural lag, but it is not integral or indigenous to his thinking and feeling. The more radical claim would be that man's responses to reality, meaning, and truth are in "self-contained, self-explanatory, and self-enclosed"[3] terms. The category of transcendence is inherently alien to the contemporary sensibility. It admits no language as meaningful which has referents beyond the concretion of what is immediately experienced. Nothing in our lived experience prepares us or enables us to be responsive to the question of God. Whatever is not self-evident is non-existent. The real is what is given and available to inspection. "A secular age, then, is one whose basic interest is with the concrete practical issues of life, without any obvious or strongly felt need to refer to any supernatural, other worldly, or ultimate realities."[4]

This secular spirit is expressed in a number of assumptions and assertions. Modern man experiences himself as "on his own"; any authority or support beyond history is inconceivable. Modern man's experience is that events have causes but not purposes; the "why" of an event can only be understood in terms of its antecedents and not a divine providence. Modern man experiences reality as change or process; an absolute or eternal is inherently inconceivable. Modern man experiences himself as the determiner of existence, the creator of values, and the source of meaning; none of this can have the character of a gift from beyond the human horizon. The secular spirit that has always existed is now utterly pervasive; it works against the possibility of speaking of God. The relevant image is not of an eclipse of God but a banishment. The present state is well represented by Langdon Gilkey when he writes: "Modern man's institutions, standards, and decisions have gradually become secular, based in his own powers of knowledge and of comprehension, and directed by his own pragmatic and immediate needs for his life, rather than on a sacred or ultimate ground given to us from beyond. Moreover, . . . each of the particular elements of this mood: its this-worldly character, its sense of contingency, relativism, temporality, and autonomy, and its confinement of thought and language to the sphere of the immediately given, have been in increasing tension if not contradiction with traditional religious beliefs, ideas, and attitudes."[5]

The most obvious effect of this developing condition is that theology "can hardly go on the way it has been going."

1

KARL BARTH and RUDOLF BULTMANN
God as Revealed in Encounter

THE THEOLOGICAL "GIANTS IN THE LAND," who were somewhat conveniently tied together with the label neo-orthodoxy, no longer stand as tall in our midst. Their ways of dealing with secularity in their formulation of the faith will not serve as adequately in the decade at hand. Yet it would be quite inaccurate to imply that their systems are like an archaeological fault through which one sifts to detect interesting artifacts from the past. They are very much with the younger theologians as "our fathers in the faith." But like all fathers the dominance of their influence has begun to wane. Some rebellious sons are more anxious than others to identify themselves as a new breed of men, but even in their protests they reveal their lineage. At the very least it is with all of us as a prologue without which we cannot understand the scenario of contemporary theology. In this study we have chosen to give attention to two theologians of the first generation, Karl Barth and Rudolf Bultmann. They are representative to the extent they reveal two modes in which theologians of their era wrestled with the question of God. In subsequent chapters we will be noting briefly the

ways in which their thought interacts with the second
generation.

KARL BARTH

Not many will remember what happened on the tenth
of December, 1968. The death of Karl Barth was not the
wrenching kind of event that left men remembering
where they had been when they heard of it. Although he
was working up to the day of his death, his thought was
no longer a major force in the sense that theologians
would anxiously await the next curvature of his mind.
Yet many paused to remember one of the most enigmatic
and ecumenical figures in theology. Robert McAfee
Brown, reflecting on the theologian's 1962 visit to
America, described Barth as "a very human individual,
possessing a shrewd sense of humor, incessantly smoking
a large pipe and wearing a beret at a jaunty angle, more
interested in visiting American prisons, the avant-garde
theater and the Gettysburg battlefields than in making
the conventional ecclesiastical tour."[1] Yet he was the
theologian of the church par excellence and many remembered on that wintry day after he had died in his
sleep that this man was without equal in his time. Only a
devoted cadre developed a taste for his way of doing
theology; that was the way Barth wanted it. But none
could deny the prodigious knowledge of the Christian
tradition and the faithfulness to Scripture which he
brought to bear upon the theological task. The intensity
of his influence ended before his life, but only an ill-
informed few will deny him his place among the master
theologians of the ages.

Karl Barth's dominant thesis is that God is his own
witness and he alone creates the possibility of man's

knowing the deity. Our knowledge of God comes from God and is on his terms; our knowledge of the world is of no value as a preparation for faith or a support of it. The true theologian and man of faith is not a mountain climber who spikes his way to the summit. He is, rather, the one who acknowledges in faith "the divine ingression." No amount of worldly erudition or intuition can be the pieces out of which man constructs a picture of God. If God is known, it is because he has made himself known.

Yet it would be false to conclude from this that theology for Barth involves some kind of immaculate conception. His own mature reflections are a testimony to the degree Barth's thought was influenced by events of moral, political, and sociological dimensions. "One day in early August 1914 stands out in my memory as a black day. Ninety-three German intellectuals impressed public opinion by their proclamation in support of the war policy of Wilhelm II and his counselors. Among these intellectuals I discovered to my horror almost all of my theological teachers whom I had greatly venerated. In despair over what this indicated about the signs of the time I suddenly realized that I could not any longer follow either their ethics and dogmatics or their understanding of the Bible and of history. For me at least, nineteenth-century theology no longer held any future."[2] While the knowledge of God comes from God, the theologian in the way he does theology bears the footprint of events to which he is a witness. Karl Barth spoke out of a very definite historical context, but he did not derive his knowledge of God from it.

It is the peculiarity and distinctiveness of Barth's theology that every doctrine is seen through the prism of Christ and that every event is grounded in the activity of God through Jesus Christ. By him the universe is created as the theater for God's dealings with men, through him the very being of God is revealed, in him God's purpose for man is revealed, by him a claim is made and a promise fulfilled. In this same focus, Barth interprets the creation of a relationship between God and man. Election takes place through Jesus Christ. Through the event of his Son, God chooses man as the object of his love. Because he is God himself and man himself, Christ is in the unique position of being able to mediate between the two. "In Him God stands before man and man stands before God."[3] Through Christ, God declares himself for sinful man and sinful man for himself.

Thus the two natures of Christ enable him to be both the electing God and the elected man, the giver and the recipient. As the electing God he is the one beside whom there is no other and through whose self-determination the election of man takes place. In no way can we "look around" Jesus Christ to an electing act of which he is not the content and meaning. Following the Gospel of John, Barth reminds us that Christ was in the beginning with God; even the decision to create was through Christ. This union having been established from the start, it is now impossible to thrust a wedge between the Father and the Son. Christ is the elector of man because all election is in Christ. In Christ we are concerned with the electing God himself and not some mere object of divine good pleasure. Through him God turns toward man.

But this same Christ is also the recipient of the divine act. "The eternal divine decision as such has as its object and content the existence of this one created being, the man Jesus of Nazareth, and the work of this man in His life and death, His humiliation and exaltation, His obedience and merit."[4] The divine decision for man comes to rest upon Jesus Christ. He is not one of the elect, but the elected one through whom all others are chosen. This does not simply mean along with him, in his company, or together with him, but "in His person, in His will, in His divine choice, in the basic decision of God which He fulfills over against everyman."[5] Thus to participate in Christ, believe in what has happened through him, is to be a recipient of the election which comes from him and to him at the same time. As others share in his humanity by faith they share in his exaltation into fellowship with God.

Christ is both the subject and the object of election; the one from whom it comes and the one to whom it is addressed. This event includes within it simultaneously the election of the community and through it the individual. A community is chosen whose function is to summon the whole world to faith in Jesus Christ. Men are not elected as private persons, but through "a fellowship elected by God in Jesus Christ and determined from all eternity for a particular service."[6] This community provides in a provisional way the natural and historical environment of the man Jesus Christ. It is provisional in that it points beyond its own existence to him by whom and for whom and through whom it lives. The community is the mediating or middle point between the election of Jesus Christ and the election of those who have faith in him. It is the witness to what God wills and has done and it is the place where it is visible and effective. Here both the judgment and the mercy of God are manifest among men, not only in promise, but in reality. This community is required both for the hearing and the believing of the determination of God for the individual man who is isolated from God by his sin. It not only tells but fulfills the promise that God is for the man who is against him. "That which has been eternally determined in Jesus Christ is concretely determined for every individual man to the extent that in the form of the witness of Israel and of the church it is also addressed to him and applies to him and comes to him."[7] It is for the man in all his particularity that the self-giving of God is effective. Thus the election that takes place in Jesus Christ is through the community but for the individual human being. It is God who creates a relationship with man.

What this means in terms of our particular concerns is that only God enables us to formulate the question of God and he alone provides the data for our understanding of him. Man may indeed have an insatiable desire to bring the being of God both within his understanding and control, but Barth's reading of Scripture forbids initiatives from man which would put God in any way at his mercy. The intellect and the emotions of man have no propensity for God which can be a prelude to faith. The question of God and all authentic knowledge of him come from God himself and remain in his control. We never even seek until we are sought and when we are found it is a pure act of grace. The only input man has into his relationship to the divine is in the form of an acceptance of what has been given to him. It is in the nature of the freedom of God that he always has man's knowledge of him on his own terms.

Yet with this freedom he makes bold gestures toward us. He permits himself to be known in his historical acts; God gives himself away in his works. We can know something of the meaning of the word "God" from those points at which he is doing something in human history. What we know of God is limited to the times in which he is dealing with us as our Lord and Savior. While withholding his essentiality in its naked form he offers an understanding of himself through his deeds. Historical revelation is our access to knowledge of God in the sense that this is where he gives himself to be known. God's "godness" is an event, his disclosure of himself "has everywhere a natural, bodily, outward and visible component."[8] Pious abstractions and spiritual speculation cannot rise up to embrace his being. Human action and reaction, rationality and emotion, exercises and overtures, make no claim upon his nature. The God who lives from and by himself is known through these happenings in particular times and particular places which are loaded with his presence and activity. The form of man's knowledge of God is that it comes from God as he moves through historical events.

This action for Barth always has the character of a determination to seek and create fellowship between man and himself. He overflows in the direction of the human, is revealed in events that reflect his will to be for us and with us. God seeks and establishes unity with man. He acts as one who loves man; the action of God is the love of God. Barth, of course, does not proceed from a definition of love to its application in the case of God. He is determined to let the acts of God establish and describe the nature of love.

When we do this, Barth claims that the love of God for man has four characteristics. First, "God's loving is concerned with a seeking and creation of fellowship for its own sake."[9] The relationship willed and established has no other content and no other purpose than God's giving of himself to man. Man does not have bestowed

upon him favors, power, courage, or any of the traditional virtues or qualities. God gives himself, his presence,
and therefore everything. The only "benefit" is the "with-
ness" of God. Secondly, "God's loving is concerned with a
seeking and creation of fellowship without any reference
to an existing attitude or worthiness on the part of the
loved."[10] Man has no capacity for his love and no claim
upon it. A bridge is thrown out from one who has
everything to one who has nothing. Thirdly, "God's loving is an end in itself."[11] There is no "small print," "hidden clause," extraneous and devious purpose. God loves
because he is love and all that happens is contained in
and defined by his love. This love itself is the blessing
and the purpose of his loving. Finally, "God's loving is
necessary, for it is his being, the essence and nature of
God."[12] He is free of external compulsion. While God is
everything to himself and without needing to be more,
he wills not to be merely for himself but for man.

It is in the nature of God that he loves, wills, and
creates fellowship with the creature who has no claim
upon him. "His loving is itself the ground of his loving.
His loving has its aim and purpose in itself."[13] He who is
love reveals himself in time and space as loving. To say
"God is" is to say God loves. And for man to be a person
is to be so loved and to love others in the way one is
loved. The one who is a person in this full sense is Jesus
Christ.

What Barth has been saying here is the dynamics of
the freedom of God for man. God has freedom at the
core of his being; he lives and loves in freedom. We are
apt to spend this term for one meaning: freedom from
external compulsion. Surely he is "unlimited, unrestricted,
and unconditioned from without."[14] God is free to create,

reconcile, and redeem without reference to anything outside himself. He is a self-moved being. Thus we are ac-
customed to saying that God is free from others. But the
freedom of God also means that he is free from himself
and his freedom! "God has the prerogative to be free
without being limited by His freedom from external conditioning, free also with regard to his freedom, free not to
surrender himself to it, but to use it to give Himself to
this communion and to practice this faithfulness in it, in
this way being really free, free in himself."[15] God is not
only free from conditioning, but is free to be conditioned.
In a real sense he has the freedom to become unlike himself! This is the key to the incarnation. God can give
himself in a sphere of reality which is not himself and
be limited by the very sphere over which he is Lord. That
is the supreme manifestation of his Lordship. He is free
of his own possibilities, unlimited by his own unlimitable-
ness. The Word became flesh, lived under the limitations
of historical existence, because God is not bound by his
own essential existence. He does not need himself as he
is in himself, but can take on the form of human existence.
In saying this, however, we are not implying that God
loses himself, but that he affirms himself. God is free of
himself so that he can be subjected to the death of a
cross, but he is not even limited by taking on the conditions of limitation; there is Easter morning as proof of
that. Barth is his own best interpreter here: God can "so
indwell the other that, while He is its Creator and the
Giver of its life, and while He does not take away this
life, He does not withdraw His presence from this crea-
turely existence which is so different from His own divine
life."[16] God can rule his world in supreme majesty or in
abject servitude, as the one who is unconditioned or as

the one who is conditioned, within the limitations of his own natural laws or in defiance of them. This we know only in and through Jesus Christ, the one in whom God exercised his freedom not to be free without being defeated.

In summary, for Karl Barth the possibility of knowing God comes from the freedom of God to make himself known in historical events. In and through the event of Jesus Christ he elected man as the being who would have a relationship with him. God is the possibility of knowing God and Christ the decisive point of disclosure. There can be no approach from the side of man in his reason, disposition, or emotion. There are no categories through which man can "snag" a picture of his being. We know God in the miracle he forms in Christ. "In Jesus Christ there is no isolation of man from God or of God from man. Rather, in Him we encounter the history, the dialogue, in which God and man meet together and are together."[17] The knowledge of God begins in a relationship that God in his freedom creates. Through this taking up of humanity into deity the knowledge of God becomes a possibility for man.

RUDOLF BULTMANN

It would seem that a person at the center of controversy ought to be a controversial personality. Rudolf Bultmann is one of the most gracious and gentle figures in twentieth-century theology. When he visited in the U.S.A. a dozen years ago one theologian commented, "As Bultmann talked of his work in a quiet and unpretentious way, with meekness before his accomplishments and kindness for critics, I found it difficult to remember that

here was a scholar about whom such vicious things had
been said and whose work had been so threatening."
But it remains true that this German New Testament
scholar and theologian has had a most decisive impact
upon scholarship in this century and has provoked both
inordinate praise and intemperate condemnation. While
he took no delight in either, he proceeded with determination toward what he understood to be the necessary
theological task given to him. This was to enable a right
and meaningful hearing of the Word of God in Jesus
Christ. The way in which Bultmann works toward this
goal will become evident as we consider first the nature
of our knowledge of God and then the method of interpretation required in our time.

Essential to Bultmann's understanding of knowledge is
the premise that one must have at least some prior relationship to a reality before he can understand it. "You
cannot understand any text of which the theme is music
unless you are musical. You cannot understand a page of
a book on mathematics unless you think mathematically.
. . . You cannot understand a novel unless you know
from your own life what love or friendship, hate or
jealousy, etc., are."[18] It is necessary to have something
going for you in advance in order to attain knowledge.
There is always a prior relationship to the subject which
enables understanding and formulates the questions we
bring to the inquiry. Now this raises the issue, Does man
possess any natural knowledge of God? The answer is
negative in that no knowledge of God is contained within
worldly or human structures from which one can construct a picture. Yet man does have a preconscious relation to God which has been expressed in the classic words
of Augustine, "Thou hast made us for Thyself, and our

heart is restless until it rests in Thee." At this point Bultmann makes a very subtle and significant distinction.
"Man has a knowledge of God in advance, though not
of the revelation of God, that is, of His action in Christ.
He has a relation to God in his search for God, conscious
or unconscious. Man's life is moved by the search for
God because it is always moved, consciously or uncon-
sciously, by the question about his own existence. The
question of God and the question of myself are identical."[19] When man possesses authentic concerns about himself, he is already asking about God. It is not that the
questions are inseparable or even indistinguishable; they
are the same. It is not that man asks about his own existence and then is led to ask about the existence of God;
the two questions are identical.

The nature of the preunderstanding man has of God
is a function of the finiteness of which every human being
is or could be aware.[20] He knows himself as a being concerned with daily provision of the means of living yet
who has no means of guaranteeing his future. He knows
himself as a being with an indefinite longing for the true
and the beautiful which it is not within his power to
attain. He knows himself as a being with a desire for
love but destined to solitude, thirsty for knowledge but
limited in what he can know, dominated by a sense of
ought but unable to obey. For Bultmann, God is the mysterious power that limits man and controls his future
even when he designates himself as master. *It is God
who makes man finite,* who makes a comedy of man's
care, who allows his longing to miscarry, who casts him
into solitude, who sets a terminus to his knowing and
doing, who calls him to duty. . . . And yet at the same
time it is God who forces man into life and drives him

into care; who puts longing and the desire for love in his heart; who gives him thoughts and strength for his work, and places him in the eternal struggle between self-asser- tion and duty."[21] God is the One who bounds man and sets the limits of human existence. He is the power at the border of human limitations. He is known in the knowl- edge man has of himself as finite.

Yet this preunderstanding, this natural knowledge available to all men, is not equivalent to the Christian idea of God. It is the prior relationship to the subject and no more. In point of fact, for Bultmann what man really knows in the experience of limitation and require- ment is himself! The natural knowledge of God is no more than self-knowledge. The object of his knowing is man and not God. We ought not to read this despair- ingly, however. This very self-knowledge is the precon- dition for knowledge of God and sets the stage for the revelation of God. "Christian belief has its peculiar char- acter in speaking of an *event* that gives it this right (to speak of God), in saying that it hears a *Word* which de- mands that it should recognize God as standing over against man. For Christianity belief in God . . . [is] belief in a definite Word proclaimed to the believer."[22] God is known in response to this Word revealed in Jesus Christ and not as a result of some general human capacity or attitude. We have to do with an act or event through which it is disclosed from the other side who God is. Only then can we know who it is who constitutes the boundaries of our human existence.

But the question remains, How do we come in contact with this Word? How do we get beyond our preconscious knowledge to the real thing? Obviously it does us no good to know Jesus Christ as the past. One cannot go back and warm one's hands by a history that is not one's own. The event of God must be present. This comes about in proclamation. "Christ meets us in preaching as one crucified and risen. He meets us in the word of preaching and nowhere else."[23] The act of God now is the Word of God proclaimed to me now. In preaching the event is present, the deed of God is for me and to me in this moment. True faith in God arises not from our preconsciousness (although not without it) but from the Word which has been heard. This hearing is not an act of knowing in which we accumulate evidence and assemble it in some sort of convincing way but it is a decision before and because of what we have heard. Faith in God is a commitment. It is the decision that we will live for the future and against the closure of the world. We have faith and awareness in every moment when we stand for the possibilities that are open to us in God. In such moments we accept ourselves, not in terms of the world's securities and promises of safety, but in terms of a man in Christ. We are free for the future and free from the past. That is the event of God now which transpires through preaching when it is heard by faith.

This focus upon preaching directs us to the problems of interpreting Scripture. Our access to the Christian understanding of God through Christ is by way of the Biblical records. Yet, paradoxically, the God who revealed himself in the Word made flesh is rendered inaccessible by the very document which witnesses to this event. This leads Bultmann into the program known as "demythologizing," a method of existential interpretation that seeks to enable us to hear what is contained and concealed in the thought patterns of another time.

In an early and intensely significant essay, we are introduced to this problem in all its boldness.[24] "In the fullness of time" God sent his Son "to redeem those who were under the law." He became "flesh and dwelt amongst us full of grace." Though he was without sin himself he came "in the likeness of sinful flesh and for sin." In his death there was "an expiation by his blood, to be received by faith." This death was not final in that Jesus was raised and "exalted at the right hand of God" where he reigns "until he has put all enemies under his feet." One day he will come again in the clouds and we will be drawn up "in the clouds to meet the Lord in the air." There ought to be enough here to suggest that Bultmann has hold of a real problem! This is simply not the orbit in which our speaking and hearing is carried on! And it would be only at some sacrifice of truthfulness that we could enter into this framework of thought and faith.

Professor Bultmann reduces this problem to its bare essentials when he identifies its origin in the New Testament picture of the world as mythological. The Biblical writers inevitably and inescapably couched their message in terms of how they understood the world. For this they are not to be criticized. They, like the writers of every age, had to deliver their message in the outlook and images of their times. But we cannot now expect modern man to accept a world view he knows to be untrue. We should not be surprised that with his rejection of the world view of ancients goes a rejection of the message which they would proclaim. If a truthful reality were given us in a form that did not conform to what we know to be true, we would likely be suspicious if not immune.

Our task then is to find a way of proclaiming the saving action of God in Jesus Christ without the mythology of the first century. But first we need to be clear on what we mean by myth. If our inclination is not to accept it as literal fact, it may be to dismiss it as a fairy tale. When one says, "That's a myth," the implication is that it is a lie; we must be done with it and get down to the facts. But this is not a fair interpretation of myth as it is found in the Biblical records. Here myth is always an attempt to speak of something not of this world in terms that are of this world. For better or for worse, we have no language appropriate to God and his dealings with his world. All we have at our command are words and images that "fit" our human experience. Thus we are constrained to use language befitting one realm to speak of another.

What we need to understand is that "the real purpose of myth is not to present an objective picture of the world as it is, but to express man's understanding of himself in the world in which he lives."[25] Through the use of myth man can give expression to his faith that the origin and meaning of the world lies beyond it, that he stands in it as one who is not his own God, and that there is one who can deliver him from forces over which he has no control. Thus while myth is necessary as a means of talking about the transcendent, it must also be recognized that it inevitably impedes this process. In a sense you cannot get along with it and you cannot get along without it.

This leads us to the task as Bultmann outlines it. He is rather careful to suggest that he is not concerned with selection or subtraction. It is no more helpful to sort out certain dimensions of the Christian proclamation than it is to eliminate others. The task is to interpret, to find a way of getting inside the mythical thought forms without ignoring their necessity and without assuming their literal validity. For this process the term demythologizing has been chosen. This might appear to mean that we are going to strip the Christian message down to bare essentials and free it from any imaginative and poetic language. Bultmann distinguishes himself from the liberal school in that he defines his project as interpretation. He is not interested in reducing the Christian faith to a hard core of propositional truths. He is concerned to penetrate the verbiage and imagery of faith so that modern man may be confronted by the saving meaning of the Christ event.

The problem with our approach to myth in the past is that we have investigated it cosmologically; that is, we have in effect asked after its truth as a picture of the world. On these terms it is clearly unacceptable. The Russian cosmonaut was quite right when he came back from his flight in space and announced he had not seen God. Only if one took seriously the ancient view of the world would he be expected to. For Bultmann, the authentic way to approach mythology is anthropologically; that is, to see it in terms of what it says about man's understanding of himself. What a person ought to bring to myth is not natural science's description of the world but man's own questions about himself as a being in the world. The key to understanding is not the objectivity of the laboratory but the subjectivity of one's living with himself. Myth points to the truth about man and not empirical facts about the universe. And the way for us to understand a particular text is to ask what the author is reflecting about his own existence and in turn what this means for my understanding of my life. This puts the reader in the position of having to make a personal decision about whether or not he will appropriate the message of the writer.

Now we are able to see how Bultmann conceives the

problem of speaking of God and where he departs from the program of Karl Barth. Both operate as theologians of revelation; they theologize out of the Word incarnate in Jesus Christ and attested to in Scripture. The knowledge of God is an act of God; it is not the result of any development in human knowledge or the refinement of a human apparatus for knowing. Something new has entered the history of humanity which comes from beyond and could not have been anticipated, discovered, or contemplated. The Word enters into our world as an event. While they part company on the nature and interpretation of myth, the primary divide in their thinking is elsewhere. Barth contends that we must inquire directly about God and share in the knowledge God has of himself. Statements about the God revealed in his Word are made without reference to ourselves. Although it is not possible to "keep our distance" and be objective in this sense, our subjectivity is not wrapped up in our knowledge of God. The encounter with God in his Word leads us to confession, adoration, and proclamation of God as he is in and by himself. Bultmann argues that God can only be spoken of in view of man. More specifically, I talk about God with my particular self as an active agent in the process. The individual brings himself with himself to the understanding of who God is. Man is not passively receptive but with the particularity of his being is aggressively involved in the knowing act. One cannot and ought not silence his subjectivity. This is not to be read as a limitation. In an essay on interpretation Bultmann writes, "The 'most subjective' interpretation is . . . the 'most objective,' that is, only those who are stirred by the question of their own existence can hear the claim which the text makes."[26] Assertions about God can only

be made for Bultmann as a function of our understanding of ourselves. And there is a preconscious relation to
God in man's understanding of himself. But the object is
man and not God. The Christian understanding of God
comes through his Word revealed in Jesus Christ. Our
present access to that event is preaching. In proclamation
the act of God in Christ is present to us.

In the Introduction we argued that Barth and Bultmann were not so persuasive now as they had been. The
problem centers in that they began from a base now
questioned with a stringency that had not previously
existed. Barth, Bultmann, and others of their era assumed
that the divine-human encounter was secure. They presupposed at least some degree of relationship between
God and man and proceeded from there. The secular
spirit of their day allowed for that. In quite different
ways these theologians judged that their constituencies
had the capacity to be responsive to talk about transcendence. They assumed one could talk about the acts of
God as they are known in faith; the reality of this divine-
human encounter did not require legitimizing. It was a
given; as long as this was operative Barth and Bultmann
were persuasive. But a rift began to deepen between the
language of faith and the theologian's apprehension of
his own existence. "Younger clerics and theologians began to wonder if they were talking about anything they
themselves knew about when they spoke about God, of
his mighty acts in history, of an 'encounter' with him, of
the eschatological event, and of faith. Do these words,
they asked, point to anything *real*, or are they just words,
traditional symbols referring more to our hope than to
experienced realities."[27] This brings us back to the distinction between "validity" and "meaning." A second

generation is having to face a challenge both from their environment and from within themselves! Is it meaningful to speak of God? The issue of validity is not open for debate until this is resolved.

The new direction in which the question of God must move is to ask, Where in our lived experience does God become real? This is not to assume the elements of transcendence but to explore our experience for what Peter Berger calls "signals of transcendence." In the following chapters we will consider six men who theologically are of the second generation even if chronologically this is sometimes a misleading image. Our first exploration will be into Dietrich Bonhoeffer, who began in the peak of neo-orthodoxy's influence to anticipate the secular spirit that now dominates the scene.

2

DIETRICH BONHOEFFER
God as Worldly and Powerless

DIETRICH BONHOEFFER'S LIFE ENDED in the Flossenbürg extermination camp, April 9, 1945, only days before American troops liberated the area. For his participation in a plot to assassinate Hitler, Bonhoeffer had been labeled an "enemy of the state" and incarcerated in the camp at Tegel. During the two years of confinement he wrote an assortment of letters and notes which were to have a dominant effect upon younger theologians for at least a quarter of a century after his death. He seemed to anticipate sooner and more perceptively than most the directions in which theology would have to move. In his formulation of the faith he was generally sympathetic with the prevailing theological traits of his time. Although he remained independent of all theologians, he was particularly influenced in his early years by Karl Barth. Bonhoeffer's friend, biographer, and the guardian of his works, Eberhard Bethge, writes that "when he was nineteen and already in his third year of study, he was spellbound by the theology of the early Karl Barth."[1] That influence persisted. Although Bonhoeffer's first book suggested that theology would have to begin not in the doctrine of God (as Barth insisted) but in the doctrine of the church, Barth referred to the book as a theological gem. While he was critical of men like Bultmann and Barth, it could be argued that Bonhoeffer never broke in any decisive way with them. Yet, paradoxically, he may have contributed more than any to an awareness that their theologies would become less persuasive. For this reason we see him as a transition figure who retained kinship with his mentors but also bred into theology strains that were to alter it decisively.

When we press against Bonhoeffer the question, "Where in our lived experience does God become real?" responses emerge on two levels. First, we are directed to the world as the locale of this experience and the manner of God's presence as powerlessness and suffering. Secondly, the form of transcendence as we experience it in the world is defined by Christ as a life for others; solicitude for the neighbor in need is our relationship to God.

The distinctive contribution of Bonhoeffer, however, was not so much to provide a new interpretation of the gospel as to call theology to attention before the kind of world in which the gospel would have to be interpreted. Had he lived he might well have contributed more to the former task; the latter task he performed while in prison, although there is considerable evidence he was on to the problem before that time. Bonhoeffer's significance for our present study is the way in which he identified the context within which the reality of God would have to be formulated. In *Prisoner for God*, his letters and papers written in prison, we have the "outline for a book" he intended to write after the war.[2] It would have yielded in more systematic form the material which we must now discuss; in the absence of this treatment we are dependent upon fragments that are enormously suggestive but also for their very fragmentariness subject to misinterpretation.

In his formulation of the context within which theology must operate, Bonhoeffer emphasized the theme "The world come of age." On the surface it might appear to embrace a throwback to the Enlightenment's optimism which infected theology. Nothing was further from Bonhoeffer's mind. No man who had witnessed the demonic in Nazism could have written that illustrious phrase from a prison camp and meant that things were getting better! Bonhoeffer does not use "world come of age" as a value judgment but as a description of a situation or condition; it is not intended to suggest that things are improved or improving. Adulthood marks the time of accountability and responsibility. Adults are no "better" than children, but they are more in the position of having to take hold of things and bear the burden of them. No adult is self-sufficient, but he has gone beyond the point from which he can absolve himself of responsibility.

The maturity of the world for Bonhoeffer meant simply that it had to be read and responded to on its own terms. To understand its workings men need no longer impose sagas of the divine. Righting the wrongs of the world is not to be looked for as a responsibility emanating from the heavens. The worth and meaning of life does not await participation in another life later on. Man is responsible and accountable in a world which has its own reality. Escape into piety is not an option. "There is no longer any need for God as a working hypothesis, whether in morals, politics, or science."[3] It is neither possible nor desirable to interpret one world in terms of another. This

world can and must be understood on its own terms. The
maturity of the world is the time in which it has been
"de-divinized." It cannot be relegated to or interpreted
with the concepts of absentee deities who run the opera-
tion from the front office. Man himself must accept responsibility for the order of the world insofar as possible.
Bonhoeffer's point, of course, is not that this phenomenon
ought to take place but that in fact it is taking place.
Man's knowledge through science and his ordering of
things through technology have rendered obsolete a view
of the world that encourages men to sit back and wait for
the gods to act. A metaphysics or a theology that assumes
that the world is still in its infancy simply is not "with it."
Bonhoeffer's concern is that the Christian faith be articulated in an awareness of "the world come of age" and
this is seen as the will of God rather than presumption.
He wills the autonomy of man and the world. In fact,
"God allows himself to be edged out of the world and
on to the cross."[4] While man attempts to use God as a
deus ex machina, God refuses to be that entity whose
power man invokes to do for him what he can do for
himself. It is the powerlessness God has elected for
himself which sets man on his feet and enables him
to accept, interpret, and utilize the world on its own
terms. It is intellectually dishonest and morally degen-
erate to depend on God. Man is left to his own devices in
the world with only the powerlessness and suffering of
God as his accompaniment. "The world come of age"
demands that man, as the form of his faith, live fully and
unreservedly in this world accepting his duties within it
and the agenda that it lays before him. This world is not
normative for his faith but neither must an antiquated
faith become normative for his understanding of the

world and his place within it. Such a faith was never
Biblical and the maturity of the world has preempted
its viability.

A correlative theme is religionlessness. Bonhoeffer had
learned from Karl Barth that religion is a form of unbelief. It is the attempt of sinful man to commend his
own goodness and secure the services of God. Bonhoeffer
refined and intensified that critique by saying that religion is the device by which men avoid their maturity
and the demands of faith. "Bonhoeffer pictured *religion*
as any human activity to reach salvation or the postula-
tion of a deity for help, protection, or explanation, in
order to underscore the nature of *faith* as active participation in the suffering of the world which discerns God's
presence in the 'nearest Thou at hand.' "⁵ He perceived
the religious interpretation as the attempt "to speak on
the one hand metaphysically, and on the other individualistically."⁶ By speaking metaphysically he meant using
the God-hypothesis as an explanation for the world that
completes what man cannot otherwise know at the time
and securing oneself in a world view that affords an
escape from responsibility for the world. One might call
this "enclave religion." By speaking individualistically he
meant a preoccupation with one's personal salvation. He
argued that in the Old Testament there was no concern
for saving one's soul and that in Romans the righteousness of God alone is affirmed. In religion man's inwardness is at the center and God is confined to the borders of
existence. Man then proceeds to neglect his worldly
responsibility.

Once again we discover that Bonhoeffer is not merely
talking about the way things ought to be but the way
they are becoming. "We are proceeding towards a time of

no religion at all: men as they are now simply cannot be religious."[7] Modern man no longer needs religion. He can find whatever answers he needs elsewhere and has ceased to be concerned with making good in some afterworld. What Bonhoeffer saw developing was a removal of the "linchpin" in the way Christianity was being interpreted. The premise was being repudiated that man is inherently religious. The day when the "*a priori* 'premise' simply does not exist"[8] is a real possibility if not the case already. Man is becoming "radically without religion" or religionless. That base for expressing the reality of God, Bonhoeffer saw as atrophying.

In his treatment of religion Bonhoeffer is contending both that it is disappearing and that it is a distortion of the Biblical faith. But this confronted him immediately with a new problem: finding a religionless manner in which to interpret the Biblical concepts. Obviously this meant taking seriously the adulthood of the world; it precludes using God in relation to our deficiencies. Bonhoeffer agonized with this problem in a meditation on the occasion of a baptism. He reflected upon how the ancient words pronounced over the child would be perhaps equally an enigma to the baby and to the adults who heard them. "Atonement and redemption, regeneration, the Holy Ghost, the love of our enemies, the cross and resurrection, life in Christ and Christian discipleship— all these things have become so problematic and so remote that we hardly dare any more to speak of them."[9] These have been rendered meaningless by a scientifically and technologically oriented culture. He goes on in the baptism piece to call for "a new language, which will horrify men, and yet overwhelm them by its power. It will be the language of a new righteousness and truth, a language which proclaims the peace of God with men and the advent of his kingdom. . . . Until then the Christian cause will be a silent and hidden affair, but there will be those who pray and do right and wait for God's own time."[10] Unfortunately, Bonhoeffer did not live to fill his own prescription.

With the concepts of the world come of age and religionlessness, a martyr over twenty-five years ago defined the context within which many theologians would be operating for decades to come. He understood the need to accept the world on its own terms without an escape into false piety or the imposition of a foreign world view. At the same time he predicted the demise of religion and analyzed its incompatibility with faith. With these tools Bonhoeffer did not intend to undermine Christianity but to clear the way for the revelation of God in Jesus Christ.

He understood that the time was coming, indeed had come, when mention of the word "God" made men uncomfortable. The cluster of meanings around it was sufficient to deny God! He confessed that in the presence of religious people he would shrink from mentioning God by name while on occasion he felt free to speak openly of God to nonreligious people. The reason was predictable: "Religious people speak of God when human perception is (often just from laziness) at an end, or human resources fail: it is really always *Deux ex machina* they call to their aid, either for the so-called solving of insolvable problems or as support for human failure—always, that is to say, helping out human weakness or on the borders of human existence."[11] His frustration was that he could not make the word mean what he felt it was intended to mean in the Biblical faith among those who thought they knew what it meant!

But what kind of relationship to God is Bonhoeffer advocating? It can best be expressed with the paradox, living without God before God. In his own words, "The God who makes us live in this world without using him as a working hypothesis is the God before whom we are ever standing."[12] To live without God meant for Bonhoeffer the determination to do what is required of us in any given situation, to work things out on our own terms. There is no need to invoke a deity to cope with our burdens or solve our problems. Men do quite well without God and that is what God wants them to do. Indeed, God forsakes us in order to accomplish this end. Man is entitled and required to assume responsibility for himself and his world without recourse to higher powers. Yet he is invoked to live before or with God. Deprived of the God-hypothesis as a device to "get along" he is free to assume an authentic relationship to God. In the "outline for a book" Bonhoeffer spoke of it in these terms: "Our relation to God [is] not a religious relationship to a supreme Being, absolute in power and goodness, which is a spurious conception of transcendence, but a new life for others, through participation in the Being of God."[13] To live with God in the world, and not attempt to leap over the world to God, was the only authentic form of faith for Bonhoeffer. And that meant more precisely to live for others, the form of life in Christ. With this model of living without God before God in view, we can examine more precisely several concepts that expand its meaning. One of the more illusive and necessary is the powerlessness of God. This is written against the hypothesis of Western theism as it appeared, for example, in Descartes. As Paul van Buren writes: "Descartes' God is too big. . . . The God of Descartes . . . was the God who could do anything, literally do anything in or about this world. He was unambiguously omnipotent."[14] Bonhoeffer affirmed a God who was weak in the world, but this weakness was the form of his power. He preferred the power of powerlessness to the weakness of powerfulness. "God is weak and powerless in the world, and that is exactly the way, the only way, in which he can be with us and help us. . . . Man's religiosity makes him look in his distress to the power of God in the world. . . . The Bible however directs him to the powerlessness and suffering of God; only a suffering God can help."[15] This is the meaning of the cross. God did not come in glory and lay claim to a worldly throne. He was born in a stable and died on a cross. For Bonhoeffer it was the suffering and powerlessness of Christ that made God real for him. One can speculate that the whole prison experience was instrumental in making vivid for Bonhoeffer this dimension of the Biblical faith. In that context it was a cruel illusion to think of the religious God who solved insolvable problems. What was meaningful was faith in the God revealed in Christ who was with him suffering in the world.

Bonhoeffer had no need or desire to protect God from the world. Following the Biblical tradition he affirmed radically the worldliness of God. With his understanding of the weakness and suffering of God he was recognizing God decisively in the world where he wills to be. He argued against those religious forces which purified God in some abstract system or incarcerated him in some mystical piety. He abhorred all attempts to draw God back into a spiritual or conceptual realm where he would be safe—and where we would be safe from his demands! It was the world God loved and the world into which he entered. Nothing offended Bonhoeffer more than a theol-

ogy that pushed God out to the borders of life. "God is
the 'beyond' in the midst of our life";[16] his place is not
on the outskirts of the village but at the center of it. He
relates to man not primarily at the point where he is giving out but at the center of his life where he is coming
on strong. God lives and acts in concreteness in the midst
of where life really is. His is the power of powerlessness
in the real world, at the heart of men's affairs.

Now we are in a position to consider a most decisive
feature of Bonhoeffer's understanding of the relation of
God and man in the world. But before we do that it will
prevent creating a distorted picture of this theologian if
we remember that he was a man with a rigorous commitment to spiritual discipline as preparation for participation in the world. This was not a retreat into the individualism he deplored or the inwardness he saw as a
false approach shot to God. It had nothing to do with
saving the soul for the next world; it had everything
to do with equipping himself for his responsibilities in
this world. In *Life Together*, for many Bonhoeffer's most
important book, we witness his concern for the life of
devotion. The chapters on the day with others and the
day alone are without equal in literature of this kind
written in the twentieth century. Bonhoeffer was a man
of piety without being pietistic. He was a worldly man
but intensely Biblical about his worldliness. While we
have said he did not bypass the world to get to God,
neither did he bypass God to get to the world. "For Christians the beginning of the day should not be burdened
and oppressed with besetting concerns for the day's
work. At the threshold of the new day stands the Lord
who made it. . . . Therefore, at the beginning of the day
let all distraction and empty talk be silenced and let the
first thought and the first word belong to him to whom

our whole life belongs."[17] And lest we think that private
and corporate acts of devotion were only viable before
his prison writings, we can remember that in the camp
he did not shrink from the functions of pastor. It is reported that he ministered to inmates and guards alike.
An English officer wrote: "Bonhoeffer . . . was one of the
very few persons I have ever met for whom God was real
and always near. . . . On Sunday, April 8, 1945, Pastor
Bonhoeffer conducted a little service of worship and
spoke to us in a way that went to the heart of all of
us. . . . He had hardly ended his last prayer when the
door opened and two civilians entered" and summoned
Bonhoeffer. They all knew that this meant the gallows
for Bonhoeffer. He took aside the Englishman and said,
"This is the end, but for me it is the beginning of life."[18]
Those who attack Bonhoeffer as a man who has sold out
to the secular would do well to remember those words
and deeds which reflect the secret discipline of the man.
It was acts of devotion that pushed him into the world.

Nothing was more important to Bonhoeffer than genuine worldliness. This was not, as some of his critics
argue, an absolutizing of the world. Bonhoeffer was too
shrewd a theologian and too profoundly influenced by
Karl Barth to fall into the trap of making the world another god alongside God. Worldliness is the accompaniment of religionlessness. It means taking the world seriously on its own terms. But it also means accepting the
world as the place where God is and makes his demands
upon us. God is, to be sure, transcendent. Bonhoeffer was
secure enough in the "Godness of God" to stress his
radical imminence. The event of Jesus Christ is that concrete revelation in which God sealed his covenant with
man and the world. Whatever we know of God and whatever we mean when we use the word "God" is revealed

in that event. We can neither mount the world for an
assault on God nor mount God for an assault on the
world. We have the two together in revelation.

But more specifically, the experience of transcendence
is to be found in the concern of Jesus for others. As
quoted earlier, we do not have a religious relationship to
God as an absolute power but a new life for others which
we understand in Christ. And this directs us to whatever
needs to be done in a given moment as the form of our
relationship to the transcendent. "The transcendence con-
sists not in tasks beyond our scope and power, but in the
nearest thing to hand. . . . [This is] a life based on the
transcendent."[19] The life and way of Jesus is radical concern for the other in need as he is present to us. Jesus
is the man for others and to be a man for others is our
experience of transcendence. Here it becomes clear that
Bonhoeffer is rejecting the idea that there is a sacred and
a profane which we can know apart from one another.
When we share in Christ we participate at one and the
same time in the reality of God and the reality of the
world. "There are, therefore, not two spheres, but only
the one sphere of the realization of Christ, in which the
reality of God and the reality of the world are united."[20]
We shall not find God apart from the world or the world
apart from God as a result of the Christ event.

The significance of this is that "the unity of the reality
of God and of the world, which has been accomplished
in Christ, is repeated, or, more exactly, is realized, ever
afresh in the life of men."[21] The Christian is one who
cannot withdraw from the world but is drawn into the
world in the manner of Christ as a man for others. The
world does not separate him from Christ, nor does Christ
separate him from the world. The Christian takes his
place in the world after the style of Jesus. To live before

God without God means to exist for other men. God has
defined man's relationship to himself and the world
through the relationship of Christ to both. He who would
know God must participate with him in the sufferings of
the world. God is forever in human form, "the nearest
Thou at hand."

   It would probably be fair to say that Bonhoeffer on the
problem of God is of more diagnostic than programmatic
significance. This is not a function of his capabilities as a
theologian but of his untimely death. Had he lived he
would surely have answered in a more comprehensive
way the question that came to preoccupy him in prison:
How can we speak of God in a secular way? Yet we ought
not minimize his contribution toward this end. He did
clear the way for a Biblical understanding of God and
the world. Bonhoeffer's treatment of religionlessness certainly purged much of theology of its pietistic and metaphysical ways of escaping the world and laying on to
God the burdens of man. He liberated many from the
tutelage of a false deity which made man less than man
by making God more than God. And surely the worldliness of God in Christ restored a balance to theology
which the excesses of men like Karl Barth had obscured.
Bonhoeffer stressed the imminence of God in a way that
protected his transcendence but restored him to his place
in the world and his accessibility to man. To know God
as "the nearest Thou at hand" is about as immediate as
one can get. It may be that Bonhoeffer's most significant
contribution was to make the case against the God of
religion. But he did cause an about-face in the onward
march of theology by acknowledging that the place of
God is with men in the world and that the role of man is
obedience to the claim of God in the neighbor. The reality of God and man as it happened in Christ is repeated

or realized ever again in the lives of men. Christ goes on happening at the heart of the affairs of men. The beyond is in the midst. On that tart claim the reality of God is based.

It is difficult to appraise the contribution of Bonhoeffer for several reasons. Certainly one is that the manner of his life and death rises up to give increased credibility to his thought. On principle one should separate ideas from their origin. We know it is unwarranted to discredit them by tracing them back to their source; it ought to be unfair to accredit them by being unduly influenced by the circumstances of their origin. Perhaps we need not immunize ourselves against our emotions in this crass a manner. Bonhoeffer lived his faith under radical circumstances and in a radical way. That says something for the viability of his theology; it does not, of course, say everything. But we are also faced with a dilemma in appraising his work because of its fragmentary nature. As Paul M. van Buren has observed, "Where his theology becomes really interesting, it is preserved in only bits and pieces."[22] Men of quite different bent have claimed him as their patron saint. Many have said that the fragments from prison are not representative of his thought in general. Karl Barth goes so far as to suggest that they reflect a mind suffering enormous pressures and are not to be taken seriously. Others have postulated the two Bonhoeffer hypotheses; before and during the prison episode we see two quite different theologies. Such is the burden of the fragmentariness of his late writings. How can one be critical in any responsible sense when it is not absolutely clear or agreed upon what the man is saying?

Yet we do not need to be paralyzed by these limitations. Clearly he administered some much-needed antidotes to the trends of theology in his time; yet he never

broke decisively with them. Bonhoeffer learned his les-
sons well on the place of Scripture; his thought to the
very end was Biblically informed. He never reduced
Christ to a good man to be admired but kept in focus
the act of God in the first century; his theology is Christo-
centric. While he was critical of the church he never
ended his love affair with it; he understood it as Christ
existing in the world as a community. In all these and
other ways he was influenced by strains within neo-orthodoxy. Yet he tightened the screws upon it as well. Karl
Barth's emphasis upon the otherness of God was challenged by Bonhoeffer's emphasis upon his worldliness. In
attempting to save God from identification with strains
of culture in liberal theology, Barth drove him out of
the reach of man. Bonhoeffer drew back His presence
with a more imminently oriented posture. He also argued
that Barth's narrow view of revelation made "a law of
faith,"[23] which functioned much like religion. From his
Biblical emphasis he saw Barth hardening into a take-it-
or-leave-it dogmatism. Bonhoeffer checked the enthusiasm
of Bultmann's disciples for the process of demythologizing. He warned that it was a throwback to the old liberal
tradition of reduction. Myth, he claimed, is not a garb
for universal truth; "this mythology (resurrection and so
on) is the thing itself."[24] Bonhoeffer also protested that
the existential interpretation represented a form of individualism. The lonely self asking questions of itself never
is able to take seriously the world for which it is responsible. It can be seen from these random illustrations that
Bonhoeffer retained kinship with men like Barth and Bultmann but served as a corrective. What is probably most
significant is that he bred into the theology of his time
a repudiation of religion and an accent upon worldliness
that undermined its viability.

In the light of this it is relevant for us to return to the question, Where in our lived experience does God become real? Clearly it is a question to which Bonhoeffer was responsive in a way his mentors had not been. But, as Langdon Gilkey contends, Bonhoeffer's contribution to this new direction in understanding the reality of God is ambiguous. He appears both to assume the security of the divine-human encounter and undermine it with his claim that the world has come of age and Christian symbols have become meaningless within it. If Bonhoeffer is the transition figure we have assumed, it is not surprising that we should find elements of the older tradition alongside new elements struggling for ascendancy. Gilkey reflects this ambiguity when he writes, "Although this writer believes that Bonhoeffer himself probably retained the centrality of the vertical dimension of faith in relation to God . . . nevertheless, some of the things he *said* in his latest writings could be interpreted as a rejection of this whole religious or vertical dimension of Christianity in favor of action in and for the world."[25] The least that can be said from this is that Bonhoeffer induced theologians to take seriously their lived experience in the world as they deal with the reality of God. His contribution was more in the form of creating an awareness than providing an alternative to the way in which his predecessors operated. This is what leads Schubert Ogden to claim that what Bonhoeffer "offers in the way of a constructive statement about God is so insufficiently developed conceptually that it presents no clear alternative to the traditional theism that it is intended to supplant."[26] Bonhoeffer pointed theologians in a new direction, but his own hints and contentions cry out for clarification and amplification. Perhaps what must be said is that Bonhoeffer taught us to live with the right question but cannot fully satisfy our need to know how. That we understand the world as come of age and God as present in weakness and suffering while our response to the neighbor is in the form of our relation to transcendence is indeed an important point of departure. It does not leave us, however, with a sufficiently developed understanding of the reality of God "to supplant" the theism of tradition.

It is apparent that Bonhoeffer's later work has led to a wide range of responses, the most recent and prominent has been the "death of God" movement. More often than not these reactions have taken off from the phrase "The world come of age." It is both central in Bonhoeffer's thought and particularly susceptible to abuse. No man can be held accountable for the distortions of his thought, but it is significant when a dimension of a man's theology is misappropriated consistently. Paul Lehmann, a fellow student of Bonhoeffer's in the United States and a judicious interpreter of his thought, has said that "the phrase has . . . functioned as a misleading half-truth, carelessly and sometimes capriciously disseminated. As such a half-truth, 'the word come of age' has supported the sloganizing of 'the death of God.' . . . Bonhoeffer has been caricatured as the apostle of Christian atheism, the troubadour of the new optimism, the Saint George of the post-Christian era whose sword of the secular spirit has decapitated the two-headed dragon of tradition and transcendence."[27] Certainly much of this can be attributed to the fragmentariness of the record. But there is the possibility that the concept lends itself rather adroitly to the alleged distortion. Bonhoeffer himself struggled to maintain the dialectic of faith and worldliness. Yet his legacy at this point may be productive of distortions. The phrase does function as a "misleading half-truth." "The world

come of age" may be dangerous more for what it leaves
unsaid than for what it says.

It is not altogether clear what distinctions can be made
between worldliness in Bonhoeffer's theology and the
classic demand for relevance. Certainly his inner motive
was to preserve that dimension of the faith which took
the incarnation seriously and saw the place of God in
the world. But one is moving on less secure territory
when he then proceeds to a genuine worldliness for
man that causes him to accept the world on its own terms.
This need not absolutize the world, but it may tend to
extend its authority beyond boundaries that should be
respected. At this point we must use Bonhoeffer against
Bonhoeffer. In an earlier piece he had warned about the
concern for relevance and what it does to the faith. "But
where the question of relevance becomes the *theme of
theology,* we can be certain that the cause has already
been betrayed and sold out. . . . The intention should not
be to justify Christianity in this present age, but to justify
the present age before the Christian message."[28] Of
course, Bonhoeffer does not use the term "relevance"
and does not press toward that goal. But there is the possibility that he creates the same effect when he affirms
worldliness and calls upon man to read the world on its
own terms. It may not be that this world which has
"come of age" should purge Christianity of its distortions but that Christianity should purge "the world come
of age" of some of its illusions. The point need not be
labored, but on Bonhoeffer's own terms must be pon-
dered.

Bonhoeffer's call for a "non-religious interpretation of
Biblical concepts" and for a secular way in which to
speak of God also raises some question. As one of his
more perceptive interpreters writes, "It is much easier to

grasp what he meant by 'religious' than 'nonreligious'!"[29] Certainly he wanted the faith to be understood as a demand to live radically in the midst of the world, "taking life in one's stride, with all its duties and problems, its successes and failures, its experiences and helplessness. It is in such a life that we throw ourselves utterly in the arms of God and participate in his sufferings in the world and watch with Christ in Gethsemane."[30] This is the direction in which he would have the Biblical concepts drive. They are to be interpreted in terms of responsible involvement in the world. Metaphysical and individualistic terms cannot perform that function, he claims. That is why he calls for nonreligious interpretation. The issue becomes fuzzy, however, when we ask what this new language will sound and read like. And while Bonhoeffer saved God-talk from being relegated to abstract systems and the inwardness of man, is not worldliness a potential trap? Does it not as well provide categories alien to the gospel? Much of our apprehension on this point might be removed if we had an example of nonreligious interpretation from his own pen. Bonhoeffer's thrust was in the right direction when he called for nonreligious interpretation, but we may need to be saved from it as well.

The problem with Bonhoeffer's theology is often that in the hands of lesser men of faith it has its vulnerabilities. But as a much-needed corrective, he taught us to love and respect the world after the manner of God. And then that this love and respect was the form of our faith in God. Knowing who he was, Bonhoeffer knew where he belonged; his death was seal and signature of that. Living without God he suffered with God in the world and by his weakness broke down the powerful.

3

PAUL M. VAN BUREN
God as Meaningless Discourse

PAUL M. VAN BUREN EMBRACES THE ANALYSIS of this age
provided by Dietrich Bonhoeffer and takes up the task
of a secular interpretation of the gospel. The meaninglessness of Christian verbiage today, which Bonhoeffer
reflected in the piece on Baptism, is the backdrop against
which van Buren performs his theological responsibilities.
We no longer look to a transcendent realm where our
longings will be fulfilled and our problems will be solved.
For both theologians, modern man is not a phenomenon
apart from and over against the Christian man; he is
within the Christian as well as the secularist. Part of the
kinship of the two theologians is in this fact and that they
both experienced themselves within the faith yet in need
of new ways of expressing and interpreting it. Van Buren
speaks approvingly of Bonhoeffer: he "wrote as a citizen
of this modern, adult world, as much inclined as the next
man to consult the weather map and the meteorologist
for the answer to a question about a change in the
weather, rather than to 'take it to the Lord in prayer.'"
He refused to immerse himself in a "Christian ghetto of
traditional formulae"[1] for the purpose of preserving faith.

The need both men understood is to find a secular understanding of the gospel for secular man who is himself
committed in the Christian orbit. It is faith seeking understanding, not an apologetic task in behalf of the un-
believer, that animates their efforts.

Van Buren's response to our concern with "Where in
our lived experience does God become real?" is to say
"Nowhere." When secular man examines his experience,
he finds it wanting with respect to absolutes. His lived
experience and conceptualizations of it preclude even
asking about the reality of God. There is no meaningful
way in which we can even use the word. On the constructive side, van Buren calls for a secular interpretation that
centers upon Jesus and the effect of his radical freedom
upon us. That is something of which our lived experience
is supportive.

While van Buren took over the analysis of the situation
from Bonhoeffer, he radicalized the problem when he
proceeded to follow his own agenda. He goes well beyond the dialectic of faith and the world, religionlessness
and worldliness. "The world in which I live . . . is a world
which I should like to describe as following upon, or in
the last stages of, a major socio-psychological shift in our
culture, which I shall label 'The dissolution of the Absolute.' . . . [This means] the passing of a world view and
a habit of thought. . . . People no longer seem to operate
on the assumption of an absolute."[2] We must now do
theology, van Buren argues, not only without the benefit
of absolutes but also without using words and concepts
drawn from a time and scheme where the absolute had
a prominent place. With this van Buren makes an assumption somewhat far removed from Bonhoeffer; and
he also proposes a method alien to Bonhoeffer's. This

is linguistic analysis that attempts to clarify the meaning
of statements by examining their ordinary usage.

Protestant theology has been on to the issue of the
language barrier to the Christian message for some time.
We were exposed to this in our treatment of Rudolf Bultmann and his program of demythologizing. His attempt
to release the transcendent from its encapsulation in the
mythological thought of another time through existential
interpretation was a creditable gesture in the right direction, according to van Buren. But he addressed himself
to modern man outside the church, whereas van Buren
claims to be interested in an interpretation for the man
of faith seeking understanding. In addition, he loses the
historical basis of faith by virtue of the existential interpretation which lays such stress upon the individual and
his contemporaneity. Perhaps most importantly, Bultmann proceeds as if it were still meaningful to speak
of God. Van Buren acknowledges, however, that existentialism has made a significant contribution but it does not
reflect the dominant temper of our culture. Theologians
who appropriate existential analysis draw upon a language alien to men "whose job, community, and daily
life are set in the context of the pragmatic and empirical
thinking of industry and science."[3] With the possible ex-
ception of times marked by unusual personal crisis, the
thinking of men reflects a culture that is pragmatic and
empirical. Van Buren's contention is that Christian discourse must be transacted within the empirical categories
of our scientific and technological age. This means, specifically, employing the method of linguistic analysis. He
is quick to differentiate this from logical positivism. The
contention in this movement is that there are only two
kinds of meaningful statements. One is a formal statement of logic and mathematics which is true by defini-

tion. The other is a statement whose meaning can be verified by appeal to empirical data. This defines all theological statements as meaningless; they cannot be called true or false. This verification principle sets theology in limbo where the only honest thing to do is ignore it.

Linguistic analysis is of another bent. The concern here is with the function of language, how words and statements are used. And it proceeds from the more liberal assumption that there is a variety of types of language each of which might have a different kind of credibility. The same word may perform different functions in different types of sentences. Appropriate canons of verification must be employed. "There is no reason why one should look for the same sort of evidence for a biologist's statement concerning a certain experiment and a statement of love by a lover."[4] We cannot in all instances expect the same kind of data to count for or against all "language games." We must look at words and sentences in context and on their own terms. This is a significant modification of logical positivism which brings all language to the same court for accreditation or rejection. The significance of this for Christianity is not that it can prove its truth or falsity but that it can set it to the task of speaking more precisely and clearly. Linguistic analysis intends to exorcise those "language cramps" which prevent our saying or implying precisely what we mean.[5]

The heart of van Buren's method is that the meaning and use of a word are identical.[6] To know the meaning of a statement or a word, we have to be attentive to the way in which it actually functions. This means that in forging a secular interpretation of the gospel we must examine the context within which the language of faith has been spoken. Theological statements were made by particular people at particular times for particular rea-

sons. We cannot understand the meaning of the words
"Jesus is Lord," unless we determine the reason a person
spoke or wrote them. "We shall have to ask why they
were said in a given situation, what they were intended
to accomplish. The function will vary to some extent with
the context, and as it varies, the precise meaning will
change."[7] In one context a believer may be reminding
himself of a basic faith commitment or perspective.
Another context may find a believer attempting to indicate to someone that he has this commitment and not
another. Two different and related functions are involved;
they are not identical. Words or sentences are meaningful when we can verify them by what they are doing.

When we apply this modified principle of verification
to the problem of God, van Buren proposes a breakthrough of sorts. The attempts of Bultmann and others
have faltered because "the difficulty [is] not in what is
said about God, but in the very talking about God at all."[8]
There is no way in which we can tell how the word is
being used. The substitution of other words like "ground
of being," as in Tillich, does not solve anything because
we do not know how that new phrase functions. Existential analysis, as in Bultmann, may tell us something about
ourselves but nothing about what the word "God" means.
Van Buren is not calling in question the existence of God.
He is calling in question the question of God. There is
no data that will count for it or against it. While we
obviously can use the word, the use of it cannot be speci-
fied. There is no possibility of verification. The most it
can do is express human attitudes and perspectives. The
only productive alternative is to translate God-statements
into language about man which is the course van Buren
pursues.

To highlight this we can call attention to the distinction

between cognitive and noncognitive statements. A cognitive statement is essentially objective; it is a statement about reality and does not include the feelings about it or attitudes toward it of the writer. There is empirical data that can be appealed to for its verification. A noncognitive statement is a perspective on reality rather than representations of it. It suggests a way of viewing what is. As such it is highly subjective and can only be understood by attention to the stance of the writer. It cannot be verified by attending to the data of reality but the data of the person's own living. The truth of the statement is either confirmed or denied in the behavior of the author. The word "God" is not cognitive; it does not tell us anything about reality. There is no empirical way in which the word can be tested. When it is used it expresses a feeling or attitude toward life. When I say "'God'" I am expressing the way in which I look upon reality. But this is confusing because it is implied that I am talking about something that has a reality of its own and can be attested to empirically. Therefore it is a misleading reference and the concern for precision in communication commends to us the dropping of the word from our vocabulary. Our task, according to van Buren, is to translate God-statements into man-statements. They are open to investigation and therefore verification. The word "God" must be dropped from our vocabulary. As a cognitive statement it is meaningless and as a noncognitive statement it is misleading. Let us then, argues van Buren, talk about "bliks" or perspectives on life since statements about God are indirect ways of expressing human attitudes and feelings.

Van Buren has precluded references to God in his secular interpretation of the gospel and seeks a humanistic language composed of noncognitive statements that

remain faithful to the New Testament and the church
fathers. That is a substantial order, perhaps more than
can be delivered. But he proceeds courageously toward
this goal, confident that Christianity is fundamentally
about man and not about God. "Its language about God
is one way—a dated way, among a number of ways—
of saying what it is Christianity wants to say about man
and human life and human history. . . . What Christianity is basically about is a certain form of *life*—patterns of
human existence, norms of human attitudes, and disposi-
tions and moral behavior."[9] From within a given community of faith this way of perceiving man and his condition has emerged. That community came into being
as a result of Jesus of Nazareth. Christianity is a function
of the style of behavior and the perspective on life of
that man.

Rather than engage in meaningless talk about God,
van Buren engages the story of Jesus as the center of
Christianity and the heart of the Christian message. He is
aware that considerable suspicion surrounds the attempt
to rest one's case on the historical dimension of Jesus'
life. One can no longer construct a life of Jesus; the
records do not lend themselves to that kind of activity.
But, van Buren argues, this does not mean we have to
concentrate on the message to the exclusion of the historical roots of Christianity. "The kerygma [essential
message of Christianity] took in part the form of telling
the history of Jesus, and the history itself was told as the
good news."[10] We have sufficient data for reflection;
examination of it yields a Christian perspective.

What this reflection and examination yields is the fact
that Jesus was a remarkably free man. His behavior, his
spoken words and parables, and the reactions of others

to him all witness to this freedom. Van Buren deserves
to be quoted at some length on this point. "Although he
is presented [by the Evangelists] as a faithful son of his
parents, he is also shown to be free from familial claims.
He followed the religious rites and obligations of his
people, but he also felt free to disregard them. . . . He
was called rabbi, teacher, but his teaching broke down
the limitations of this title. . . . He called his hearers to be
without anxiety for the future concerning clothes, food,
or shelter, and he supported his words with his own con-
duct. Perhaps the most radical expression of this freedom
is found in an incident in which Jesus forgave a sick
man his sins, and then demonstrated his right to do this
by healing him. . . . He seems to have been so free of any
need for status that he was able to resist all attempts
by others to convey status on him. If we would define
Jesus by his freedom, however, we must emphasize its
positive character. . . . He was above all free for his neighbor. . . . He was free to be compassionate for his neighbor,
whoever that neighbor might be, without regard to himself. The tradition reveals . . . his openness to all whom
he met, his willingness to associate with those whose
company was avoided by respectable people. He was reported to have taught that the greatness of freedom lies
in service, and his own freedom was characterized by
humble service to others. . . . He was, apparently, a man
free to give himself to others, whoever they were. He
lived thus, and he was put to death for being this kind
of man in the midst of fearful and defensive men."[11]
These are the results of a historical study of Jesus as a
man.

But van Buren recognizes that this historical knowledge is not the same as faith. This picture of a man was

not the basis of faith even in his own time. Although his
disciples gave up much to follow him, showed evidence
of loving and trusting him, they all fled when he was
arrested. Jesus as a man did not effect in his disciples
the freedom he had in himself. "His freedom was his
alone."[12] It must be concluded then that the Christian
faith is not a direct result of a historical figure in the first
century. Yet it can be said, paradoxically, that Christianity is based on history. It has an indisputable foundation
in history. Had the events been otherwise, had Jesus, for
example, spent his remaining days in the wilderness to
save himself from the cross, Christianity as a faith would
never have come into being. Van Buren comes to the
conclusion that "faith is not based simply on a picture of
the historical Jesus, but the historical Jesus is indispensable for faith."[13]

This riddle is exposed in a careful reading of the
Easter stories. The resurrection of Jesus from the dead
is not an event that is open for exploration. We cannot
submit it as such to verification. But we can approach
and examine it from the context of the lives of those
who said, "He is risen," or reported that they had in one
way or another seen him. The behavior of one particular
witness, Peter, is available to us. It is possible for us to
see what it meant in his life. It would seem that Peter,
and the others as well, experienced a new discernment.
After Easter they looked on the historical life of Christ
in a different way. While they had formerly seen his life
as a failure, they now perceived it as a key to the meaning of their history. From this viewing of the historical
life there emerged in them a commitment to it. Peter's
Easter faith is validated in the eyes of van Buren in that
Peter also, "according to an old and probably reliable

tradition, died on a cross."[14] While we can say nothing about what happened on Easter in the usual sense, we can say that then and there the disciples began to share in the freedom of Jesus for others. On Easter, Jesus had what he had not possessed in his lifetime: the ability to awaken freedom in others. It became "contagious" in a way it had not been before. Van Buren is not saying that Easter is merely a subjective event. Something was experienced by the disciples. All that we can say of it meaningfully, however, is what it meant in the lives of the disciples. They began to live as liberated men. Thus the secular meaning of the resurrection is that one begins to experience himself as caught up in the freedom of Jesus and the secular meaning of his Lordship is that one commits himself to live the freedom revealed in the life and death of Jesus. This is the "historical perspective" of the disciples and of all true Christians. They tell and live the story of a free man who set them free. Jesus as liberator is the point from which they see the world and live in it.

When a Christian confesses the Lordship of Jesus, there are two dimensions to this phenomenon. One is an exclusive strain in his commitment. There is a contention of universal significance for a particular historical being. While Jesus embodies remarkable freedom, it must be acknowledged that there have been and are other free men. They may indeed have a liberating effect upon others with whom they have contact. The gospel is more than a story about a free man; "it is the good news of a free man who has set other men free, first proclaimed by those to whom this had happened."[15] In the context of the proclamation it has happened again and again for nineteen centuries. In response, men have accepted this

liberator as the one who defines their humanity and provides the point from which they orient their lives. Their
understanding of themselves is controlled by their understanding of Jesus. The firmness of this conviction and the
way in which men have lived it is its verification. It has
empirical ground in the context of the existence of those
who confess it. The claim of exclusiveness for Jesus has
validity because we can follow it up and see that it works
in real life. Those who confess Jesus as Lord are saying
that they get their freedom by being free in Christ and
nowhere else.

But they are also saying that this faith or perspective
they have upon themselves and from which they view
the world is not just the result of a decision they made
one day. It was something that grasped them and held
them in its truth. In the gospel, faith is something given,
it is a response drawn from man, and therefore not an
occasion for boasting. The logic of the language of faith
is not that I have made up my mind about something
after considering certain options but that I was taken by
this perspective as the understanding of myself and my
orientation to the world. It is not that the believer does
something but that something is done to him. Man does
not select Jesus as his liberator but is selected by the
liberating effect of Jesus upon him. Freedom comes to
man from beyond him not from within him. A man "in
Christ" is one who has been grasped by the freedom
of Jesus and is freed by it to live for others. It has become
his perspective in its own power. Those to whom this has
happened find that they cannot contain the confession
within the confines of their lives. In the confession that
"Jesus is Lord" this perspective is articulated and the
hearer is invited "to see Jesus, the world, and himself

in this same way and act accordingly."[16] One's commitment to the way of Jesus includes commending it to others.

In summary, the Christian is one grasped by a man of remarkable freedom. He has experienced with the disciples the contagion at Easter. For him this event has become a situation of discernment which has reoriented his perspective. This historical perspective he commends to others is the secular meaning of the gospel. All talk of God has been eschewed. It is not meaningful discourse. There is no lived experience to support it. Theistic references have been translated by the modified verification principle into statements that describe and commend a particular perspective on the world, others, and oneself and the nature of the life appropriate to that perspective. The norm is the events in the life, death, and resurrection of Jesus. For van Buren the Christian faith is to be understood and represented with due accord to the empirical temper of the time and the demand for worldly involvement in the theology of Dietrich Bonhoeffer.

Paul M. van Buren sustains quite different responses to Barth and Bultmann. Karl Barth, of whom he was an early disciple, receives harsh treatment. Van Buren admires the attempt of Barth to relate to the Scriptures and the church fathers in the doing of theology. Yet he repudiates the attempt to immunize theology against modern thought in order to obtain the gospel in its purity. This he sees as an attempt to set back the clock and therefore a crude interruption of the theological task. Barth does not understand that the old thought forms are no longer meaningful and that attempts to rejuvenate them are futile. The modern empirical temper will not tolerate traditional language that has not been converted into humanistic discourse. Van Buren's treatment of Bultmann is quite different; he is the recipient of extensive consideration and strong criticism. He is attacked for losing the historical base of Christianity with his existential interpretation; he is criticized for his determination to stick with transcendent references; he is castigated for failing to recognize the empirical temper of modern man. Yet one suspects that the time and labor expended in *The Secular Meaning of the Gospel* on Bultmann and his critics is an indication of respect. It is just possible that van Buren has to move them around in order to find room for himself between them! He and the Bultmann school certainly overlap in the determination to convert the gospel into statements about man.

Paul M. van Buren is clearly one of the two or three most promising younger theologians in America. Langdon B. Gilkey's statement about *The Secular Meaning of the Gospel* is probably as judicious and insightful as any. He refers to the book as "good," "important," and "irritating." "It is good because it is original—one of the most genuinely creative theological efforts to appear in a couple of decades—and because its main thesis is clearly and powerfully presented. It is important because it addresses itself in a new way to the most crucial theological problem, namely the nature and extent of Christian language in a secular age. The fact that it is at the same time irritating *may* be because it so radically challenges as meaningless and so impossible most of our usual forms of Christian discourse—or it may be because the presentation of this rebellious thesis is neither as careful nor as tight as it might have been."[17] The least that can be said is that van Buren explores new territory and does so with considerable skill.

Much of the criticism of van Buren centers on his commitment to empiricism, especially as it is expressed in
linguistic analysis. Some of this is blunted by the fact that
van Buren picks as his model a very sane form of empiricism. "The empiricist today is not liable to say 'Show
me' at the sound of every word, nor even at the end of
every sentence or paragraph. He does, however, expect
that the whole network of his understanding . . . should
'touch base' in sense experience at important points."[18]
What is required in this view of empiricism is not that
every word be "nailed down" but that there be some
grounding of the discussion in experience so that it is
accessible to verification. This "soft empiricism" is one
in which van Buren says he feels "at home" and "makes
sense" to him. It is certainly an intriguing and responsible
position. Yet it raises some serious questions.

Thomas W. Ogletree, associate professor of constructive theology at the Chicago Theological Seminary, has
held up one issue that is perplexing from within the context of what van Buren declares he intends to do. Having
denied the viability of logical positivism with its narrow
view of meaningful discourse, van Buren claims he is
going to engage in an application of the procedures for
language analysis conceived by Wittgenstein. This philosopher of language was determined to avoid a procedure
that would reduce meaningful discourse to that with
either an empirical or a logical base. He argued for the
inclusion of language whose meaning is accessible to us
from the vantage point of its use in a sentence. We are
justified in employing words whose meaning can be determined from the way in which they function. Van
Buren, however, does not follow this lead when he comes
to the question of God. It will be recalled that he dis-

qualified the word "God" as cognitive because objective empirical verification was not possible. And van Buren discredited the term as noncognitive because it was misleading: in suggesting a human attitude or viewpoint the word implies that there is a referent behind it. Thus we must drop the word completely in order to speak more directly and clearly through statements about man. Having followed this line of argument, Ogletree concludes that "van Buren, in spite of his intention, has not followed Wittgenstein's suggested method. Rather than attempting a careful description of the way the word 'God' actually functions in statements of Christian theology, he resorts to a system of classification which acknowledges only two possible uses for the word 'God,' one of which is meaningless and the other of which is misleading or useless."[19] Had van Buren been faithful to his own declared intentions he should have been able to retain the word "God" and explicate its function.

Apart from this internal inconsistency van Buren is vulnerable for his exhaustive and encapsulating commitment to linguistic analysis. Langdon Gilkey affirms the contribution of language analysis to clarifying and explicating the Christian tradition but argues that more is required to resurrect or re-create meaningful Christian discourse. Indeed, to the degree a theology limits itself to exploring the usage of words it is particularly restrictive. Words that are meaningful to a given person are those which have a felt and usually shared relationship to experience. They thematize and symbolize what it is we know to be most real about our experiencing in life. At one time traditional religious discourse did precisely this. It was deeply and persuasively related to felt realities. But this is no longer the case. Gilkey charges that "if our description of the secular spirit has been correct, then it is precisely the sort of language we are calling 'religious' which is *not* ordinarily used and which does *not* communicate in the secular context."[20] Modern man does not employ religious language to explicate those portions of his lived experience which have immediacy. If he uses religious language, it is more on behalf of memory than present experience. But, ironically, language analysis is applied to the very words to which he has no lived relationship. It cannot make a significant contribution at the level of meaningfulness because religious discourse in our time is not functioning as a symbolization of felt and shared experience. Thus the application of language games may increase clarity but does not relate to the issue of meaningful language. To put the problem another way, the usage of religious language which we are given in this secular culture does not mean anything significant and therefore to probe it in hopes of discovering its meaning is futile. For linguistic analysis to make a major contribution by itself it would have to have access to words that were working meaningfully in the culture in order to expose through usage what in fact they mean. The point is "that no *secular* analysis of the usages of religious modes of speech is possible, since there are 'given' to us almost no such usages."[21] It does no good to see how words are functioning in sentences if they are not functioning meaningfully in life.

One of the most interesting and moving aspects of van Buren is his treatment of the freedom of Jesus. Perhaps it is particularly effective in commending this historical figure because freedom and liberation have been overpowering concerns in recent years. Jesus interpreted as a remarkably free man gives him an accessibility to the

ethos and aspirations of our age not equaled in most
theologies. Yet critics like Harmon Holcomb, professor
of the philosophy of religion at Colgate Rochester Divinity School, have been quick to argue that the problems
created by this picture are substantial. When Jesus is
defined by his freedom, it assumes that the Gospels present us with considerable evidence about his interior
reactions. Holcomb notes that "Rudolf Bultmann has re-
minded his New Quest descendents that we do not know
any of these things [about Jesus' inner life] to be true on
the basis of historical research. Bultmann claims that *qua*
empirical historians, we do not know the motives of Jesus
in going to Jerusalem, the inner attitudes with which he
faced death or the meaning he placed on his own death."[22]
The Gospels report events and their meanings to the
Christian community; they do not take us inside Jesus
and provide evidence from which we can make claims
about his freedom. While van Buren is professing to be
working from empirical data when he speaks of the freedom of Jesus, Holcomb makes clear that this is not a
question that can be resolved empirically.

Secondly, is the category of freedom sufficiently inclu-
sive and comprehensive to exhaust the full meaning of the
Christ event? Holcomb holds up to us the possibility that
this category may indeed wrench the Biblical meanings
that van Buren associates with it. Has he provided, asks
Holcomb, "functional equivalents" of the Biblical and
patristic tradition or rather marginal transliterations?[23]
Have we exhausted the meaning of the Biblical claim,
"He is risen," when it is interpreted to mean that with
the Easter event the disciples experienced the contagion
of Jesus' freedom and knew it to be true of themselves?[24]
Is saying that God raised up Jesus the same as saying that

Jesus has become one's liberator and the point from which he views the world?[25] When the church fathers and the councils said "very God of very God" in reference to Jesus, did they mean more than that the Christian sees the true nature of man in the perspective of being free for others?[26] When Paul says that "God . . . did not count their trespasses against them" (II Cor. 5:19), does he mean any more than that our perspective on others is that we should treat them as in some sense pardoned in the freedom of Jesus?[27] It is possible that in committing himself so exhaustively to one category for interpreting the meaning of Christ, van Buren has wrenched the Biblical witness and tradition to a form at least partially alien to them. It is obvious that what one brings to the gospel one takes with him. It is not possible to come empty-handed, but it may be desirable to have a relaxed grip on what is to be found there.

The Achilles' heel in van Buren's position may be exposed with the Biblical claim that a man cannot serve two masters. Van Buren has attempted to be faithful both to the Biblical and patristic tradition and to the empirical temper of modern culture. Can one be orthodox and empirical at the same time and to the same degree? As Gilkey points out, "In certain respects these two Lords turn out to be opposed to one another."[28] Surely something has happened to the Christian witness which had no reservations about speaking of God when that is ruled out as meaningless or misleading by the canons of linguistic analysis. Bonhoeffer's claim that one should not bring the gospel to this present age but this present age to the gospel for judgment certainly is relevant. It would appear that van Buren has done the former. As Gilkey charges, "The 'logic' of theological language that van Buren has found in this work is merely the logic of his own contemporary *secular* understanding of the Gospel, *not* the logic of the older Gospel itself nor of the patristic period."[29]

For van Buren nothing in our lived experience enables us to speak about the reality of God; language about God is meaningless and misleading discourse. Christianity is the story of a remarkably free man whose freedom is contagious. From its proclamation we may be freed for others. That is a secular interpretation of the gospel resulting from applying tools of linguistic analysis.

4

SCHUBERT M. OGDEN
God as Perfect Becoming

"HOWEVER ABSURD talking about God might be, it could never be so obviously absurd as talking of the Christian faith without God."[1] With that crisp judgment Schubert M. Ogden dismisses those who in their enthusiasm for the world have presumed to preempt it of the Biblical God. He is the central theological problem with which we have to struggle now and always. "Faith in God of a certain kind is not merely an element in the Christian faith along with several others; it simply *is* Christian faith, the heart of the matter itself."[2] It clearly is the case that there is a need for a new formulation of the reality of God; yet it must be remembered that it is always the formulation and not God that is problematic. Ogden would reverse the edict of van Buren: It is not talk about God that is the heart of our difficulty, but what is said about God. With the proper and available conceptual tools we can resurrect the meaningfulness of references to the divine. The alternative is to say that theology is not possible at all.

Schubert Ogden works with the question, Where in our lived experience does God become real? on two levels.

First, he argues existentially that man has an interior awareness of worth, value, meaning, and significance for which God is the objective ground. Secondly, he proceeds conceptually to explicate the reality of God as a process of perfect becoming. God is a living, growing reality to whom man makes a difference. Before we develop this position, we need to see why Ogden believes that God is at the center of theological discourse now.

While concern for the reality of God is always central, what factors constitute the particular dynamics of that issue now? Ogden contends, first, that we are victims of the liberal movement in theology against which neo-orthodoxy was a reaction. It was the greatness of liberalism to embrace secular methods of knowledge. It introduced to the study of Scriptures, for example, historical-critical techniques that had been applied to other forms of literature with great profit. But the courageous way in which liberalism pursued this theological task resulted in a dilution of essential elements of the Christian faith. In their determination to "respect all that was valid in modern man's understanding of himself and his world, they too often proceeded uncritically and thus failed also to respect the distinctive claims of faith itself."[3] In a sense the greatness and the failure of liberal theology were at the same point. While attentive to the modern situation it also was overwhelmingly indulgent. With the reaction of neo-orthodoxy the problem of God was brought to the center of our concern once again.

Another factor, contends Ogden, was the shift in our culture from secular to secularistic. Since the seventeenth century, Western culture has been dominated by science and technology. The world picture of the scientific method and the understanding it produced of ourselves and our environment has been widely accepted. With this, the pursuit of knowledge has become a "secular affair." Religion and its institutions lost control over the quest and have been prohibited from imposing their criteria for truth upon the data. Indeed, religion itself has been subjected increasingly to the canons of science. This is secularism, the search for knowledge on the terms of a scientific methodology without deference to religious dogma or criteria. But now we see a phenomenon that can be called secularistic. In this, modern men go beyond the claim that the scientific method is the only way of gaining knowledge of the world we know through the senses to saying that sense-knowledge is the only kind there is. From secular to secularistic there is a shift from affirming a method where it is applicable to saying that only where it is applicable is there knowledge. It is this denial within the secularistic phenomenon which has done much to focus the problem of God in our time. We must speak of transcendence when the mentality of our culture expressly denies this as meaningful or valid discourse.

But the third force in bringing the problem of God to the center is more intrinsic to the historic theological enterprise. Ogden identified the issue in classical theism or the supernaturalism which has dominated the faith of the church. We see this falling apart at two points in particular. Certainly one is that it makes demands upon us that are not reasonable. While claiming that faith is consistent with reason, traditional theism requires assent to themes that are irreconcilable with what we know scientifically or historically. Claims are made without warrant and backing from the very disciplines that are most relevant to them. When one affirms that God is Creator, one must assent "to a whole series of beliefs that are now widely regarded as false—e.g., that the creation of the world took place as recently as 4004 B.C. and that man and the various animals were all created as fixed species, in no way related to one another by any evolutionary development."[4] With its claims concerning "last things" Christians have been led to affirm for nineteen hundred years the imminent end of the world. These unfulfilled expectations together with our current knowledge in science and history discredit the claims that the end of the world is at hand. In the matter of miracles Christians have held the belief that God can and will do as he pleases with man and the world, whether it is to suspend the law of gravitation or cause a fire that does not burn. One would expect that verification for such phenomena would be forthcoming from those disciplines which have jurisdiction in these areas. Yet "classical theism requires acceptance of statements about the world, about its origin or end or the happenings within it, which men are willing to accept, if at all, only with the backing and warrants of science or history."[5] For the most part our best knowledge works against them or is painfully inconclusive in their behalf. Classical theism professes to be consistent with reason yet makes utterly unreasonable demands upon us.

The other flaw is probably more fundamental and less readily recognized and corrected. This form of theism carries with it a metaphysical outlook that is at odds with what we know of reality. Everything modern secular man knows is negative evidence. In the classical tradition there are perceived to be two different kinds of reality. "On the one hand, there is the present world of becoming, of time, change, and real relations, of which each of us is most immediately and obviously a part. . . . On the other hand, there is the wholly other world of timeless, changeless, and unrelated being, which is alone 'real' in the full sense of the word and so alone worthy of the epithet 'divine.' "[6] While there exists in different philosophies a variety of ways in which these two are related, there is clear agreement that it is a one-way relationship. Man and his world are related to God and dependent upon him. But God is not in turn related to man and the world, for this would postulate dependence on other than himself. He is wholly absolute Being; he cannot be affected by man or the world and this in the last analysis makes us both unreal and inconsequential. This creates in modern man a feeling of "existential repugnance."[7] If God is indifferent to man in the sense that what we do and suffer has no effect upon him, then the reality of God is rendered irrelevant by our experience of existence. Classical theism "can provide no motive for action, no cause to serve, and no comfort in our distress beyond the motives, causes, and comforts already supplied by our secular undertakings."[8] And when we do involve ourselves in the world and experience the ultimate significance of it, there is an implicit denial of the God who "ignores" our worldly life. When classical theism affirms in its metaphysical tradition a God who is changeless, timeless, and unrelated, it posits for us a God with whom we can do very well without. This tradition has brought the issue of God into a crisis situation for Protestant theology.

In rejecting the proposal to interpret Christianity without God and identifying the flaws of classical theism, Ogden does not feel he has exhausted the possibilities for theology. Our experience as modern secular men has as its common strain an affirmation of our life here and now and our world in its autonomy. Within this it is possible to determine the reality of God for our time. A self-conscious secularity can make explicit the reality of God which is implied in what it affirms. Christianity is not something alien to man but integral to the possibility of existence. Ogden goes so far as to say that "for the secular man of today . . . faith in God cannot but be real because it is in the final analysis unavoidable."[9] It is only this claim which can be consistent with the God of the Christian faith. If God is related, he has in some sense to be integral in our experience and understanding of existence. The absence of faith in God is fundamentally a misunderstanding of existence and not a denial of God. It is "the presence of faith in a deficient or distorted mode."[10] The atheist on Christian terms is one who has applied his notion of God to something other than God. Idolatry is not a matter of ridding oneself of the presence and reality of God but an indirect testimony to that which it denies. He who denies God is really saying that he cannot reconcile the concept of God with what he believes to be true in his experience of life or that what he believes to be true about life he cannot reconcile with his concept of God. In both cases he has to reject either his understanding of life or his understanding of God. Ogden does not believe, however, that these two are inevitably at odds when properly understood. In fact, unfaith occurs where there is a misunderstanding either of God or of life.

From this premise Ogden proceeds to argue on two levels. He interprets the reality of God in terms of a "neo-classicalism" which, on the one hand, operates existentially and is based in our common experience and, on the other hand, with a conceptuality in which reality can be conceived and understood.

In his attempt to restore the word "God" to meaningful discourse, yet in continuity with the past, Ogden
begins by utilizing an insight from existentialism. This
is the premise that the meaning of religious language is
not scientific or historical but metaphysical. "Basic to this
discovery is the recognition that human experience is not
exhausted by the external sense perceptions of which science and history are in their different forms the critical
analysis. Man also enjoys an internal awareness of his
own existence and of the existence of his fellow creatures
as finite-free parts of an infinite and encompassing
whole."[11] It would be inappropriate to limit his questions
to those which can be answered by an understanding of
the data of his senses. Beyond these concerns he can
and must ask about those structures of self and world,
their ground and goal, of which he is aware as he exists
as man. He is aware in himself of a confidence in the
final worth and ultimate significance of our lives as persons. To understand fully this one of man's most important forms of reflection is to grasp the constant structure of experience through which this assurance can make
sense. The meaning of such an assertion and the conditions of its truth can only be determined existentially
or metaphysically and not under the domains of history
and science.

What more specifically is the experience of our existence which is accessible only through existential language? It is at base "an experience of worth, of value,
of meaning, of significance. . . . The foundational certainty underlying all of my experience is not only that
I am together with others in the whole, but that what
I am and what they are is significant, makes a difference,
is worthwhile. This certainty . . . is what I call basic con-

fidence in the worth of life. It is, I hold, the primal faith which is constitutive of our very lives as human beings and which, therefore, is in the proper sense the 'common faith' of mankind."[12] One cannot avoid this "common faith" insofar as he exists, because in the attempt to deny it one actually presupposes it. In the act of questioning the worth of life, for example, there is the assumption of the worth of questioning and therefore by implication the worth of life in which one can question.

Ogden then goes beyond this "common faith" to affirm that the word "God" is the "objective ground in reality itself of what I have called basic confidence in the worth of life."[13] It is not an attitude some men have but the affirmation that there is something that calls forth from us the sense of worth and significance. It is not part of my inherent equipment that evolves in time. The word "God" points to whatever it is that has this effect upon man. Of course, the problem that immediately comes forward is this: Has Ogden done any more than establish a connection between God and this trust? Does it have a referent of its own in objective reality? Ogden answers by saying that in the process of using real and reality we are presupposing something about reality or we would not ask. A mode of reasoning is involved, as is the case in every discipline, and we have to accept it or drop out of discussing religious issues. And within this mode of reasoning the word "God" is a synonym for reality when it is used to define our basic confidence. In other words, the question of reality and God are the same in the logic of religious discourse and one cannot then ask if God refers to anything in reality! If discourse is to take place, we have to accept the terms of reasoning of the discipline or remain on the sidelines, and this is true regardless of the discipline. Ogden, then, is maintaining that the word "God" functions in our lives to designate our experience of the worth, meaning, and significance of existence.

But what is the function of God? It is "to make the whole venture of human life worthwhile and to call forth in us, in *each* of us, our abiding confidence in life's worth. The relevance of God, then, is that he and he alone provides the ultimate justification for giving ourselves fully and freely to the tasks of human existence, to knowing and doing, feeling and loving, with all their terrors and all their joys."[14] The difference God makes is that he enables life to make a difference! Man contributes significantly not only to the lives of others in a way that is not isolated and therefore insignificant but also to the life of God himself. The ultimate justification of the worth of life is the difference that man makes in the life of God himself. But the functional significance of God is contingent upon abandoning ourselves to him totally as the ground of our confidence and not allocating it between ourselves, our fellowman, and perhaps God himself. In this radical trust we are released from fear and anxiety over the ultimate worth of our lives. Free from ourselves and others we are free for ourselves and others through the love of God which returns having gone full circle.

It is, of course, true that whatever functions to give life this ultimate confidence is God for that person or community. Then it may be claimed in one sense that the word "God" does not have a unique referent as it does within the Christian tradition. There are many gods else there would be no idolatry. Yet there are two qualifications. For one thing, there must be a distinction made between the profession of a person and what in fact is operative in his life. In some degree a relationship to the true God may be operative even where there is total denial or a multiplicity of loyalties. Secondly, the mark of idolatries and denials of God is that man is held in bondage. The gods who are not God never set men fully free but always condemn him to some form of servitude. They do not enable him to live within the basic confidence that he is free for and from himself and others. Constricting conditions in one form or another are present and are destructive of his possibilities. Only the true God functions as the emancipator of mankind.

The first level on which Schubert M. Ogden represents the reality of God in a neoclassical mode is by existential interpretation of religious language. This results in the claim that the word "God" functions as a referent to the constant structure of reality which we know in lived experience as confidence in the worth, meaning, and significance of existence. And God himself functions in our lives to elicit this from us. When God and our experience are properly understood, we need not reject either on the basis of the other.

The second level on which he operates is the selection of a conceptuality in which the reality of God can be conceived and understood in a viable way. As theology aspires to an adequacy that is always beyond its reach, the problem of securing the right philosophy is central. The system of concepts that can best render intelligible this reality must express adequately two characteristics. It must represent a God who is truly and decisively related to our life and to whom our actions make a difference. That which is the ground of our significance cannot be immune to the significance of our lives. Our thoughts and action must make a difference to him. If he is to be so affected by us, he must be a supremely relative reality. Yet the second characteristic that must be accentuated is that his relatedness must itself be relative to nothing and his existence not affected by what we do. There is a distinction to be made between existence and actuality. We may make a difference in the development of God's being but not in the fact of his being. The ground of man's confidence must exist absolutely or it would not have permanence. The new theism, then, requires a philosophy that can represent God as both "supremely relative and supremely absolute."[15] Traditional theism has not been able to cope with either of these themes and therefore has been productive of an interpretation that is an anathema to modern secular man.

It is the conviction of Ogden that we have at our disposal a new philosophy that can do justice both to the Biblical witness and to the secular man. It is especially evident in the works of Alfred North Whitehead and Charles Hartshorne. Through it we are enabled to understand God as primal cause and ultimate effect of the world. This philosophy begins with the principle that our fundamental concepts must have an experiential base in our experience of ourselves. The self as we know it is the paradigm for reality. It is the model by which we understand the nature of reality. Unlike classical metaphysics, which interprets with categories of substance and being that are immutable, the new philosophy operates with the self as model and interprets in social or relational terms. The self is "a process of change involving the distinct modes of present, past, and future."[16] It is forever selecting from the actual and the possible to fashion itself in creative interaction with others. The key to reality is "process" or "creative becoming."

If this is the analogy that comes from our lived experience of ourselves, we may utilize it to express the reality of God and thereby conceive him "as a genuinely temporal and social reality."[17] The fact that we conceive God by analogy to ourselves does not mean that he is just another "creative becoming" among others. In the previous discussion of God as the reality that elicits from us the conviction of worth, it was established that he is a unique reality. But the point is that Ogden is attempting to speak of God in meaningful concepts that are drawn from what is real as we know it; this does not reduce God to "one of us."

It is now possible to conceive God "as precisely the unique or in all ways perfect instance of creative becoming, and so as the one reality which is eminently social and temporal."[18] Unlike classical theism where God is conceived as unrelated and unchangeable, he is here understood as a living and growing reality who takes up into himself the actions and reactions of man. Man clearly makes a difference in and to God. He is in the process of self-creation and man can have an effect upon him. He is open to change and contingent upon others even as he is a perfect reality who is unsurpassable. There remains a qualitative difference between God and man. "*That* he is ever-changing is itself the product or effect of no change whatever, but is in the strictest sense changeless, the immutable ground of change as such, both his own and others."[19] As the eminent Self he is not the world but is in intimate interaction with it. In a sense the world is his body, his sphere of interaction. In his identity he is independent of the world but in his actuality he is identified with it. God is the perfect embodiment of creative becoming. Everything that happens is important for him, yet he is absolute in the sense that his disposition to change does not change. "God, one may say, is absolutely relative. . . . The one thing about God which is never-changing, and so in the strictest sense immutable, is that he never ceases to change in his real relations of love with his whole creation."[20] In his abstract identity God is independent of the actual world, yet in his concrete existence he is included within it and subject to it.

The God who is understood as perfect creative becoming is the ground of our confidence in the worth, meaning, and significance of life. He assures the importance of what we do in the world in his receptivity to us in his own being. We participate in his becoming. The future toward which we work has its significance in that we are participating in the future of God and not merely making sand castles that will be washed away by the waves. There is a final worth to our lives beyond the immediate significance we experience. In this way Ogden renders "intelligible our deep conviction as modern men that it is our own secular decisions and finite processes of creative becoming which are the stuff of the 'really real' and so themselves of permanent significance."[21] While neoclassical theism is attentive to this secular sensibility, Ogden also affirms that it is Scriptural.

But this raises the question of whether or not it does justice to the Biblical accounts of the place of Jesus Christ. Is this a Christian theism that he advances? Ogden argues in part by claiming that the classical supernaturalism cannot do justice to the Biblical witness at this point. With its emphasis upon the Absolute in its immutability it cannot take adequate account of the incarnation. Absolute relativity makes this possible. There is a conceptuality in neoclassical theism that is eminently suitable to express the presence and participation of God through Christ in the world. Christ in our human history is what we would expect of God, not a curious antinomy. There we see that God is in it with us and open to us with astonishing clarity.

The reality of God is represented both existentially and conceptually. We begin with an existential understanding of the basis of religious language in our common human experience. God designates our confidence in the final worth of life. But this by itself is not sufficient. A new and more adequate system of concepts is required by which we can understand the reality of God. This is provided by process philosophy which enables us to understand God as perfect creative becoming. And all of this is an enterprise sensitive to secular man. It accepts what he knows to be most true in his experience of life and articulates the ground of it in a conceptuality compatible with his understanding of reality in general.

Like Paul M. van Buren, Schubert M. Ogden has made a rather clean break with neo-orthodox trends. It is most decisive in relation to Karl Barth. His determination to separate radically the Christian faith and modern culture is repudiated by the love affair between Christianity and process philosophy over which Ogden presides as Cupid. While at times Ogden can write appreciatively of Barth, the cleavage at this decisive point is one that cannot be bridged. Ogden has devoted an entire book to Rudolf Bultmann and one can assume he takes this theologian more seriously. In the latter treatment he detects "structural inconsistency"[22] in Bultmann's demythologizing project and posits a more radical alternative. But what is more important for our purposes here is that Ogden is critical of Bultmann for failing to embrace or develop an adequate conceptual scheme to represent his existential interpretation of Scripture. His "theory of analogy, while profoundly suggestive, and even essentially correct, is too fragmentary and undeveloped . . . to enable one who shares it to make a carefully reasoned defense of his case."[23] Ogden has rejected Barth and Bultmann rather decisively. The most that can be said by way of continuing influence is that he uses Bultmann as a point of departure.

Schubert M. Ogden's contribution to the debate about God is certainly impressive and important. It provides one of the most viable alternatives to denial of discourse about God precisely because of the way in which it utilizes secular affirmation and a new philosophy consonant with what modern men understand to be true of reality. But theologians have raised searching questions about his project. One of these is to challenge Ogden's contention that he is developing a Christian understanding of God. We noted earlier Ogden's claim that his position is consistent with the Biblical tradition. Yet it is important to note the degree to which it is also independent: "The only final condition for sharing in authentic life that the New Testament lays down is a condition that can be formulated in complete abstraction from the event of Jesus of Nazareth and all that it specifically imparts. . . . Not only is it *possible* to affirm that authentic existence can be realized apart from faith in Jesus Christ or in the Christian proclamation; it is, in fact, *necessary* that this affirmation be made."[24] Carl E. Braaten, professor of systematic theology at the Lutheran School of Theology at Chicago, responds that with this kind of statement Ogden has left the ranks of those who are committed to a distinctively Christian understanding of God.

He maintains that Ogden has eliminated mythology, history, and the saving act of God in Christ from the Christian tradition. "All that remains is a humanistic philosophy of existence that finally has no need of the New Testament or the resurrection of Jesus Christ. It approaches the New Testament under the lordship of modern man, fully equipped with the knowledge of what could not have happened in history and what alone could have meaning for the modern world."[25] Braaten's contention is that while Ogden's position may be compatible with the Biblical tradition at the points it makes use of it, what it excludes in a reductionistic manner must be read as a serious departure from the whole Biblical witness.

Kenneth Cauthen, professor of Christian theology at Crozer Theological Seminary, who is generally sympathetic to process philosophy, raises an interesting question about the adequacy of Perfect Becoming to give expression conceptually to our experience. He applauds the breakthrough of Ogden and others in advancing a vision of God who is involved imminently in the social and temporal process of becoming to which all men and nature are related. "This neo-classical theism provides a way of bringing together in a coherent synthesis the sublimist insights of the philosophical and religious tradition of the west, while at the same time constituting an outlook profoundly relevant to the secular consciousness of modern man."[26] But then he goes on to question the adequacy of this to articulate our total experience; granted the reality of evil, can we talk about God as Perfect Becoming? The enormity of evil in the world suggests that there must be some impediment to God in the nature of things which he has not overcome. The primordial ground of becoming is not only the source of our final confidence in the worth and meaning of existence, but, argues Cauthen, must on empirical and existential grounds reflect and include the misery and suffering in the world. Cauthen requires an understanding of God that accounts not only for the goodness of life but for its inexorable ambiguity. "My suggestion . . . is that we consider the possibility of grounding not only the being and goodness of finite existence but also the equally real sense of the ambiguity of life in the primordial being of God."[27] In other words, there ought to be a referent in the matrix of Becoming for both the positive and negative experiences of existence. The God who strives for his own fulfillment in time experiences both suffering and triumph, both the cross and the resurrection. Cauthen argues for a vision of God as the objective referent not only for the worth, value, meaning, and significance of life but for the experience of their opposites as well. While Cauthen's proposal may not be persuasive, it does have the function of suggesting that there are flaws in Perfect Becoming as a way of understanding God.

The most serious criticism of Ogden comes in the form of challenging the validity of utilizing a natural theology in the effort to restore the language of transcendence. Langdon Gilkey questions the viability of the assumptions that Ogden and others draw upon to interpret the reality of God. Specifically, he argues that in the contemporary secular mood there is "a loss of a sense of the ultimate coherence of things which reason might delineate—the loss, one might say, of any confidence in an ultimate logos in existence generally—and the consequent confinement of thought to the immediate."[28] At the very moment when we are most in need of the powers of reason to give expression and credibility to the nature

of faith those very powers themselves are in question.
Gilkey's criticism is directed at the conceptual attempt
that Ogden makes on behalf of God-talk; it is only indirectly related to his analysis of our experience. The contemporary scene does not support efforts to develop a
rationale for speaking of God using reason as the key-
stone and assuming that there is a correspondence between reality and the way in which the mind reasons.
Reason is at least as suspect as faith. To translate traditional religious discourse into the language of philosophy
and use terms like reality, becoming, and process is not
to advance the problem of God appreciably. Ogden has
contended that in process philosophy we have terms and
categories in which the reality of God can be understood
and appropriated; this is a "prodigious philosophical un-
dertaking" but the utilization of this "right philosophy"
is an "essential prerequisite of any theological construc-
tion."[29] But this confidence in reason and the mind to
take persuasive account of our experience is precisely
what Gilkey argues is not an option in the present scene.
The assumption that the mind can know reality and give
expression to what is real is unacceptable. "One of the
main ingredients of the present secular mood can be
called its 'posture of metaphysical modesty' or possibly
the 'inferiority complex of speculative reason.' This posture represents a rejection of philosophy as a form of
genuine knowing that can proceed by implication alone
far beyond immediate experience not only to talk of the
real but the real as a coherent system."[30] While Ogden
has contended that a "right philosophy" can move us
along and enable us to talk meaningfully about the reality of God, Gilkey maintains that no matter how right the
philosophy might be, in our setting it would not be per-

suasive. Whether or not Gilkey has overstated the case is open to debate; he, nevertheless, makes one have second thoughts about the case with which Ogden utilizes the vehicle of process philosophy.

Schubert Ogden has achieved a significant breakthrough in the problem of speaking of God. His location of God in our lived experience of existence is clearly an advance over those who proceed with the assumption that the divine-human encounter is not in jeopardy. If nothing else, he identifies for secular man a dimension of experience that is susceptible to symbolization and conceptualization in Christian terms.

5

FRITZ BURI
God as the Unconditionedness
of Responsibility

FRITZ BURI IS UNIQUE AMONG THE THEOLOGIANS we are studying in that he challenged the assumptions of neo-orthodoxy in the time of its greatest influence. He called for a truly liberal theology that was not a refinement of the liberalism that prevailed in the nineteenth and early twentieth centuries but of an essentially new genre. "It seems to me, at least, that 'liberal' is the perspective from which the proclamation of the Bible must be understood today, and that liberalism is the means by which Christian faith in our time can be made viable."[1] The urgency for this new formulation was created by neo-orthodoxy's "disastrous capitulation to current nihilism."[2] What he means by this is revealed in a discussion of "the face of our time" published in 1949. He pictured it as "mutilated, terribly torn by the radical opposition of atheism and belief in revelation, of nihilism and redemption in Christ, of naturalism and supernatural redemptive history."[3] Theology and culture had allowed themselves to polarize in a way that was totally unproductive. But what was more destructive was the one matter in which they concurred fully: both held a negative assessment of human capabilities. They despaired of man's capacity for knowledge and moral responsiveness and read the substance of history without a vestige of hope or expectancy. It was this alliance between the neo-orthodox formulation and nihilism which led him to the judgment that it was "anything but orthodox" and "more avant-gardistic than the theological liberalism out of which it arose."[4] Whatever semblance of orthodoxy prevailed was a function of terminology and not of what was being said. To have championed liberalism when neo-orthodoxy ruled the day was indeed courageous and Buri assumed the role without restraint.

To the question, Where in our lived experience does God become real? Fritz Buri is responsive in both negative and positive terms. Negatively, he frees us of the disposition to limit the experience of God to events unique to the Christian tradition. The possibilities of authentic existence are everywhere available; existence itself has the character of grace and does not require a saving act in Christ. Positively, God becomes real in lived experience where man begins to take radical responsibility for himself in self-enactment. It is the voice of Transcendence that comes to man with this unconditional demand. God is the mythological expression for what stirs us up to responsibility.

With this in view we can begin to understand Buri through his critique of Rudolf Bultmann. Buri supports Bultmann in the matter of demythologizing and the interpretation of the faith in terms of existence. In his eyes Bultmann has pursued the only authentic trail toward the goal of understanding the Christian message in our time. But the problem arises in that Buri is convinced that the demythologizer thought he had reached the mark when

in fact he was only halfway home. At a particularly in-
opportune point Bultmann lost his nerve. This left him
with a logical inconsistency. While with one breath he
pronounces the benediction over myth, with the next he
affirms the saving event of God in Christ. This kerygma
is nothing less than residual mythology which itself must
be interpreted. Buri argues that the Christian message
must be dekerygmatized as well as demythologized. The
result of this inconsistency is to retain the obscurity of
the faith. For whatever his reasons, Bultmann pulled his
punches at the very point where a follow-through would
have been most productive in accomplishing his goals.
But perhaps even more disastrous is that this retention
of the kerygma in its given form leads to inexcusable
arrogance. It is claimed that with the kerygma the Christian has possibilities for authentic existence that are not
available to other men. While Bultmann may establish
common ground with philosophers and secularists on the
analysis of existence, he suddenly withdraws from serious discourse with them and announces that he has something they have been denied. Only what God has done
in Christ as proclaimed in the kerygma can abstract man
from inauthentic existence and enable him to assume
authenticity. This clutching of exclusiveness is not only
destructive but unwarranted. It is arrogant and erroneous
to make Christianity appear superior to philosophy. Buri
contends, for example, that there is no difference between
the self-understanding that the disciples experienced in
the resurrection and the liberation that philosophers experience as a result of turning from the world. If we follow Bultmann's project to its logical conclusions, we will
accept the kerygma as the last vestige of mythology which
we are better off without. The gain will be both in clarity

and in avoiding arrogance. The New Testament deals with nothing more than the possibilities for authentic existence that are open to the man who philosophizes.

Buri poses an alternative in the light of his critique of Bultmann. Standing within the existentialist tradition, particularly the philosophy of Karl Jaspers, he suggests a theology of existence that interprets the faith in terms of self-understanding. This is fundamentally no different than a philosophy of existence insofar as they are reflecting the same concept of existence. "Theology of existence and philosophy of existence have their common point of origin in the reality of existence as that authentic being in relation to Transcendence, which is neither generally provable nor to be objectified mythologically or metaphysically, but which may be received only in faith."[5] The only difference is that the theology of existence has a theological tradition which it embraces as irreplaceable. Unlike Bultmann, Buri is free to merge theology into philosophy without loss and in fact with profit in terms of credibility. Theology need not, then, be based upon an objectification of sacred history but upon its own understanding of existence. It does not take the Biblical revelation to know what philosophy and theology know of existence, but the theologian knows it in terms of his heritage. The importance of the New Testament is in the understanding of existence exposed within it, but this understanding can be paralleled by that of philosophy and articulated in concord. They arrive at the same goals by different ways. This is not to imply that there is nothing distinctive about theology, that it is dispensable. It is blessed with an incredibly powerful and penetrating body of symbolic material which it draws from the Christian tradition. For all its attenuate problems, this tradition speaks to our condition in an unprecedented manner. What man as man knows about himself in his existence is expressed with depth and efficacy through the symbols of faith. We should recognize that "the moments of birth of an historically powerful myth are seldom. As arche-types they arise out of the unconscious, are formulated by prophets in outstanding hours of humanity and grow from generation to generation."[6] The myths of faith have the capacity to move men toward authentic existence and it is the function of theology to probe them until they perform that function. Philosophers may arrive at the same conclusions but without benefit of a compelling symbol system to which man has a kind of primordial response. Buri's alternative to the kerygma of Bultmann is a theology of existence that affords man self-understanding and leads him to choose authentic existence.

Fritz Buri's understanding of grace is particularly interesting. While theologians like Bultmann have maintained that grace is something that comes to man in his sinful, inauthentic existence as an act of God in Christ, Buri specifies that grace is a part of the character of existence. While it is still a gift from God it is built into the way things are rather than a special dispensation. The manner in which the Christian experiences it is not essential to the experience. He writes frequently of "existence as grace" by which he intends us to understand that grace is given with existence and not afterward. Nothing more is required for experiencing grace than the recognition of inauthenticity and the reclaiming of one's responsibility and freedom. This was the dynamics operative in the prodigal son; he "came to himself" and returned to his father. Existence knows itself as restored to itself without external intervention. Man affirms himself in the acknowledgment he is not himself and thus may recover his authentic being. One does not need Biblical events or categories to know sin and grace; they belong to the structure of living.

It is not difficult to see why Buri is charged with radicalizing Bultmann's position. This excursion has served to indicate a substantial break with neo-orthodoxy and to suggest a theistic humanism of intriguing dimensions. It is sometimes suggested that there is a major shift in Buri's position from the matters we have had under consideration to the more explicit treatment of the problem of God we are about to examine. This may be more apparent than real. Often it is necessary for a man to clear some ground before he can build his more substantial and traditional structure. This is not to deny that there are some significant shifts away from earlier influences, but it is to suggest that there is continuity and integrity to his total work. It may be fair to think of the considerations up to this point as a prologue. Neo-orthodoxy has been assaulted and an alternative projected. Buri is now free to show his liberal interpretation of God.

The key word in this formulation is "responsibility"; the emphasis upon "existence" is still present but not dominant. The task of theology is to speak responsibly of God. This responsibility is "before the God who has revealed himself decisively in Jesus Christ. Christian theology arises out of this revelation, is indebted to it for its origin, and must again and again reflect on this . . . because of the claim this revelation makes."[7] Christian theology is obligated to articulate before the whole world the claim of what has happened for all men in this event. Revelation is entrusted to theology for the purpose of getting a hearing. It is responsible to speak of revelation in such a way that it becomes revelation for the present time. Legitimate theology is responsible both to the present world situation and to the revelation of faith. "It must speak of God in the language of its world."[8]

This dual responsibility creates a tension within Christian theology that often results in subservience of one to the other. In Karl Barth, Buri says we see an illustration of theology being so preoccupied with the revelation entrusted to it that it loses sight of the world to which it should be addressed. With his concern for purity, Barth has become a voice crying in the wilderness; he ignores the given age which is to understand revelation. This is a failure to take the incarnation seriously by one who, ironically, is serious about the incarnation. In the various forms of secular theology we see men so concerned with the world that they make it the criterion of revelation. In effect they so dissolve the revelation into the world that the world becomes revelation rather than the act of God in Christ. They make the world absolute and so humanize Christ that through him we no longer have to do with God. Legitimate theology must be oriented both to the present world and to the ancient revelation. The failure to be responsible to one pole or the other results in either irrelevance or distortion.

The problem with theologians of the right and of the left, Buri contends, is that they fail to consider the nature of the responsibility they assume when they speak of God's being or not being. The issue is "the personal responsibility of the theologian for his theology."[9] It is the theologian and not God or world who speaks in theology. The nature of personal responsibility is not that one claims to be dealing with God in this theology (Barth), or that one claims to be dealing with the maturity of the world (secular theology), but that one is dealing with himself as a theologian. A legitimate theology is one in which the theologian is made conscious of his responsibility in discourse about God and the world and assumes this decisively and unconditionally. "To be mature means to take responsibility upon oneself, to push it off on neither a transcendent world, an environmental world, nor a world to come. It means, rather, to know oneself responsible for oneself in one's world and precisely in this self-responsibility to have to do immediately with God."[10]

No one is likely to deny that it is the person as theologian who writes, speaks, thinks about God, perhaps even prays to God, calls to him, listens to him, and falls silent before him. "I am the subject of my speech, my thought, my silence."[11] In consciousness I know myself as a subject in relation to objects external to me. Of course, this consciousness can be obscured; but in the attempt to become clear about ourselves and to find ourselves we have the benefit of dialogue with others. The greater clarity we attain about ourselves in this manner the more we become aware of the degree to which in our being we have been defined by our past and our environment. "We are what we have become and we cannot slip out of our skins."[12] Yet we are forever defining ourselves by how we understand ourselves. No one can do this for me and no one can take this away from me; I remain responsible for myself. This self-enactment constitutes my personhood; as such it resists objectification. I cannot think about myself and have that identical to what I am in myself. What others think of me is not the self I am. "The genuine 'I' escapes objectification. That I am responsible, I experience only to the extent that I take responsibility upon myself."[13] This is true as well of another. One cannot prove his responsibility to a man; only he can recognize himself for the responsible person he is. The awareness of this in oneself may be given in the moments of irresponsibility. The sense of dissatisfaction with oneself and guilt over what one has become correspond to the awareness of oneself as responsible for his own realization.

Buri has led us to understand the nonobjectification of our responsible personhood. The self we are we encounter in the enactment of our personal responsibility and this we can never capture for viewing and representation before others. But with this experience of ourselves as always beyond objectification, "we experience ourselves encompassed and borne in the entire sphere of the objectifiable by a similar mystery of the nonobjectifiable . . . which announces itself at the limits of our objective knowledge."[14] In concrete moments of personal experience there is known a voice. It is not the voice of something that can be objectified in a system of thought; neither is it something whose reality can be proven. But there is at the moment of peak awareness of responsibility an unconditional demand that requires response. This is the voice of Transcendence. The voice "calls it to responsibility and discloses to it space and time . . . as the place and the opportunity for the realization of responsibility."[15] Man does not speak to himself the word that calls him to himself; neither does he recognize the world as the place where he is responsible to be or understand it as at his disposal. It is because he hears the voice that he is called to a dominionship (Gen. 1:28); he either accepts or forsakes his responsibility. Man cannot redeem himself either; the possibilities for his existence are an act of grace and not an accomplishment. The tribulation that fills his history is not within his power to control toward a goal or understand as an end. That may tempt him to irresponsibility as an out. But the worst of events he can bring upon himself or others cannot trample the voice, "Adam, where art thou?" and, "Where is Abel, thy brother?" Theology and religion are about the issuing forth of this voice of Transcendence and the human response. Inevitably they misrepresent, in the name of faith as well as atheism. They rob the voice but do not silence it. The voice calls man to responsibility, makes possible his redemption, and overcomes the events and circumstances that would extinguish it.

The theology of responsibility that Buri advocates is an attempt to locate the foundation of our speech about God in the unconditionedness of our personal responsibility. It avoids the dogmatism of the right that claims one particular event in history as indispensable to authentic existence and it escapes the secularism of the left that is uncomfortable with that history in which it occurred. Theology of responsibility is not ashamed of the events of the New Testament and is not prepared to have another contemporary substitute for it. Yet it does not maintain that this history is necessary for all as the vehicle by which they understand and realize themselves.

From this base Buri proceeds to outline what responsible discourse about God means when it is faithful to the Christian tradition. First, "Christian discourse about God can only be in connection with the revelation of Christ attested in the Bible."[16] The dynamics of this event is not something projected radically into the future nor is it a mythological speculation about the past. It is a present event that happens when men are aware of the unconditionedness of their responsibility. Its effect is to enable men to shape and understand their lives in the light of it. The meaning of this "being-in-Christ" is not so integral to the historical event of Jesus or to the immediate consequences that it is unavailable apart from the event. The Christian proclamation is the occasion for reception of the event but it can as well impede our awareness. Others have access to the personal responsibility in community through different means. As we saw in the consideration of grace, it is available with the givenness of existence and is not something the Christian faith adds to existence. Christian discourse centers in the event of Christ but it is free to appropriate elsewhere what may serve as an expression of "being-in-Christ."

Secondly, "About such a Christ we cannot speak 'without' myth because the awareness of personhood and the appeal to responsibility are dependent on mythological assertions."[17] It is the unique status of myth that while it is objective it has a kind of transparency to those matters which are nonobjectifiable. Existential interpretation does not require elimination of myth; rather, in its transparency to the unconditioned it is the proper language of Transcendence. In what must be read as a bold claim, Buri affirms that "God is the mythological expression for the unconditionedness of personal responsibility."[18] The voice by which we are called to responsibility achieves clarity through mythological discourse. Without God there is no access to "being-in-Christ"; without myth there is no access to the voice of God. The Christ-myth, however essential it may be for the Christian, is not essential for all men. While we cannot have Christ without God, we can have God without Christ. One might immediately wonder if in this reliance upon myth Buri has rejected his earlier emphasis upon demythologizing and dekerygmatizing. Certainly he is now more sympathetic to the traditional forms in which the Christian faith has been received. But the recognition of mythology even in the kerygma remains integral to his thinking. While his appreciation of myth is probably enhanced, what is important is that he sees the Biblical language as no more than myth; from beginning to end it needs to be interpreted.

Thirdly, the voice calling us to responsibility "gives us the possibility of experiencing the redeeming and creative reality of personhood as the voice of God."[19] There is no reason why we should not speak unashamedly of a personal God. By faith one knows that the voice that penetrates and summons us into our personhood is indeed the voice of one who is over against the man who hears in being led to decision and obedience. When man hears in this way he knows what redemption is, that by grace he is released from his failings as a person. He also understands creation and consummation at the same time. For him creation is "the experience occurring in one's own historicity of the unconditionedness of a creative beginning which creates order in the midst of chaotic relativities, overcoming those relativities by using them as possibilities for the manifestation of unconditionedness."[20] And for him consummation means "the awareness that one has never achieved completion of himself as a person, the awareness of the fragmentariness and imperfection of every embodiment of responsible being, the knowledge that the new creature still lies hidden in the body of the old Adam."[21] When we experience redeeming, creative, and consummating forces in the unconditionedness of our personal responsibility, we are free to speak of God as Creator, Redeemer, and Consummator. Even if these are only approximations of his reality, they emerge from our experience and glorify him. From the experience of one's own person we may speak of the God who is personal.

Fourthly, in response to the charge that this personalistic interpretation of Christian mythology may lead to ambiguities and misunderstandings, Buri grants that personhood and transcendence are not realities which in the usual sense can be demonstrated as true; neither dare one presume to speak without equivocation. Yet in the sphere of the personal, credibility is of a different order than in the objective world of science. We need to remember that "personhood in its responsible relation to Transcendence is in principle nonobjectifiable. One cannot have the truth; he can only be in the truth. In the same sense there is also no having-of-Christ in the truth but only a being-in-Christ. One cannot prove personhood; one can only appeal to it; person from person, 'through faith for faith.' "[22] Operating from within the context of the personal need not be a source of anxiety; it has its own credibility within experience and dare not submit to any other.

Fifthly, "Prayer is essentially the actualization of the unconditioned relation of responsible personhood to transcendence. Unconditionedness is the dimension in which the voice can be heard, God appealed to, and an answer given to Him. . . . The praying man has to do with a transcendence which is not silent, but which speaks to him and hears him."[23] Of course, prayer is subject to misunderstanding and distortion because of its being objective discourse but it is still "the appearance of responsibility."[24] The unconditional fulfillment of personhood inevitably entails prayer. In the last resort, responsible discourse about God emerges from discourse with God. A good theology, according to Buri, is not to be measured by its value in proclamation; responsible discourse is evidenced in its relation to prayer. To think about God is to think about, and from, the way one prays. Ultimately one knows the responsibility for which one is responsible in prayer. It is the enactment of responsible personhood.

By way of summary, God is real in our lived experience in concrete moments when the voice of Transcendence is heard as unconditional demand and asks for our response. What it asks of us is unconditional personal responsibility through which we are enacted in our personhood. God is then understood as the mythological expression of the unconditionedness of our responsibility. There is no discourse about God without mythology; for Christianity the Christ-myth is central and essential but that to which it points can be enacted without an understanding of the historical event of the first century. Grace is indigenous to existence. Christianity is a powerful myth-system that is particularly qualified to be transparent to God and to communicate an understanding of authentic personhood.

Fritz Buri is a particularly interesting theologian in our study because of the early way in which he detected flaws in neo-orthodoxy and brashly advocated a new liberalism. While it may be argued that he has softened somewhat and become more sympathetic to Christian tradition, this may be more a function of the atrophy of the opposition which he understood as literalistic than a fundamental change in his own position. Except for some obvious shifts in mentors and cherished terms, we see his work as of a piece. The early critiques on Bultmann are certainly operative and instructive throughout. Yet surely he is illustrative of his own claim that no theologian finally does the job required of him.

John Macquarrie, Lady Margaret Professor of Divinity

at Oxford, has been one of his most faithful interpreters as well as one of his most astute critics. He contends, first, that Buri's two criticisms of Bultmann are over-drawn. The charge of logical inconsistency may be more real on the surface than it is in fact. It is possible that absolute consistency is less than a virtue in the theolog-ical enterprise. Macquarrie argues "that the ambiguities in Bultmann may be more of the nature of paradoxes rather than of irreconcilable contradictions. . . . [Buri] does not seem to appreciate that paradox may be inevit-able in theology."[25] Indeed, the articulation of the Bibli-cal faith demands paradox and this is a more accurate category for what Bultmann has posed than irreconcil-able contradictions. As for the charge of arrogance in claiming too much for the Christian and the event of Christ, Buri exaggerates its impediment to dialogue with philosophers, according to Macquarrie. Aside from the fact that it could be true that the Christian in revelation has something not accessible to others apart from Christ, it is not clear that his alleged arrogance is a barrier. "It is surely absurd to maintain . . . that when a theologian accepts a *kerygma*, he is *ipso facto* debarred from the possibility of a dialogue with philosophers. That would be the equivalent to saying that a dialogue is possible only if the theologian is prepared to become purely and simply a philosopher."[26] What Buri interprets as "one-upmanship" may be the nature of dialogue in that a man has to be honest and bring to his discourse with others the full burden of his convictions. An element of dogmatism may be an asset to constructive discourse. The alternative is really complete capitulation and the admission that there is nothing distinctive about theology as a discipline.

Buri's discussion of grace is both exciting and limiting. That it might be a structure given with existence is a concept for which it is easy to generate enthusiasm. But Macquarrie counters that "Buri may well have underestimated the effects of sin in man, as alienating him not only from God but from his own authentic self."[27] The claim that grace indwells existence generally and that no special act of God is required to overcome man's self-encapsulation, Macquarrie finds at odds with the Biblical tradition. What Buri obscures is that in the New Testament "the act of grace transcends my existence and comes to me from beyond myself."[28] Now Buri might want to dismiss this claim as mythology. But by his own admission myths are powerful symbols for understanding existence and on what basis can we accept some and reject others? Furthermore, the failure to be responsive to the disabling character of sin in existence has led Buri to create a theology that is primarily for the "healthy minded."[29] Macquarrie points up the vulnerability of this in a rather commanding way. "It is certainly the case that the great leaders of the Christian Church—Saint Paul, Saint Augustine, Martin Luther, to mention only three—began their spiritual pilgrimages as sick souls who could find no way out from their difficulties, and were transformed not by any indwelling grace of existence but by the encounter with God in his gracious act in Christ."[30]

Buri's view of human possibilities and the relative ease with which they can be released may correspond more readily to those whose psychological state is euphoric at least for the moment and be an anathema to those who feel more trapped by life. Grace without the act of God in Christ may be "cheap grace" for simple sins. Many human beings are more locked in than Buri's perspective on grace would allow.

Despite what Buri has to say about the unconditionedness of personal responsibility in community, he is also
criticized for creating a theology that is too individual-
ized. The influence of existentialism marks his analysis
of existence in a way that affects its viability. Macquarrie
asks, "Does Buri, in spite of some of the perceptive
things he has to say about community, really overcome
the individualism of Bultmann and other existentialist
writers?"[31] The conviction is emerging that theology must
relate in an integral way to the social structures and conditions in which men live. We need not have a love
affair with the secular city to understand the way in
which our lives as individuals are woven by the fabric
of the social order. That itself can be absolutized until
it is a distortion, but certainly part of the modern sensibility is defined by the structural alliances men have in
society. It is not enough for God to be related to the
individual and through him to community. Perhaps
in our time it even needs to be the other way around. A
doctrine of God that does not have some explicit things
to say about community may have nothing to say to
contemporary man. The individuality of existence in
existentialism may be a fateful feature of Buri's theology
of responsibility.

Fritz Buri is only beginning to receive in this country
the reading and reaction he deserves. He develops a
line of thought that is not otherwise included in our
discourse about God. His concentration upon responsibility as the form of our relationship to God is most
suggestive. And the fact that he comes to this from exploring secular man's self-understanding opens up possibilities
of considerable import for enabling contemporary man
to speak of God from his lived experience.

6

WOLFHART PANNENBERG
God as the Power of the Future

THE TASK TO WHICH WOLFHART PANNENBERG has set himself is that of establishing the faith from public evidence. This is the form of his modernity. Christianity does not need an alliance with a particular secular posture like existentialism or linguistic analysis to be with the age. Pannenberg assumes no uniquely contemporary court within which it has to be tried. The faith can accredit itself on its own terms and those are historical. Either the gospel can achieve credibility upon examination of its history by any reasonable person or it is not to be taken seriously. Historiography and historical research are the tools with which the theologian must work and without their supportive results he may not proceed to make claims on the basis of "secret information handed down." Reason's knowledge of history, not the derivation of revelation from experience, constitutes public evidence.

Pannenberg's contribution to the question, Where in our lived experience does God become real? is to direct us initially to historical data in the first century. It is in the risen Christ attested by witnesses to the facticity of the resurrection that God begins to be known. Beyond that our understanding of God is through Jesus' message of the coming Kingdom. The Kingdom of God symbolizes that future rule of God through which he will be fully known. The reality of God is ahead of us. Our lived experience of God's present reality is as the power of the future.

On the surface there is nothing startling in the proposal that Christian theology must take history seriously. Few would dispute the claim that Christianity is a thoroughly historical religion. Obviously Jesus was a very historical figure! But recent theologies, neo-orthodoxy in particular, have not rested their case on the historical evidence. No one is more concerned with the activity of God in history than Karl Barth, and yet he writes as if the historical problems in claiming this did not exist. He sets aside the tools of historical research and proceeds to affirm the faith on the basis of God being his own witness. Rudolf Bultmann, on the other hand, is so aware of the historical problems that he removes the faith from any decisive relationship to the original events. What matters is the historicity of the believer who responds to the kerygma now. He is concerned with what is happening in our self-understanding rather than what did happen in the first century. Paradoxically, it was the characteristic of neo-orthodoxy to take history seriously without being serious about history! It could affirm the "acts of God" and make its case above the actual historical events. This in the last resort is to detach faith from its historical moorings. The effect is a loss of history as the basis and substance from which the Word of God is proclaimed and our understanding of existence determined.

Pannenberg is anxious to get the case for Christianity back out in the open. This means that we must concentrate upon "revelation *as* history" rather than *in* or *through* history. It is not something added from without or burrowing from within or even a meaning that man imposes upon events. Pannenberg teaches us that the history in which all men participate is revelatory. It would be well to have before us his own summary of the relationship between revelation and history.

Thesis 1: According to the Biblical witnesses, the self-revelation of God has not occurred directly, after the fashion of a theophany, but indirectly through his historical acts.

Thesis 2: Revelation happens, not at the beginning, but at the end of history.

Thesis 3: Unlike special manifestations of God, historical revelation *is there* for anyone who has eyes to see. It is universal in character.

Thesis 4: The universal revelation of the Godhead of God was not yet realized in the history of Israel, but first in the destiny of Jesus of Nazareth insofar as the end of history occurs beforehand in him.

Thesis 5: The Christ event does not reveal the Godhead of the God of Israel as an isolated event, but only so far as it is part of God's history with Israel.

Thesis 6: The universality of the eschatological self-disclosure of God in the destiny of Jesus was expressed by using non-Jewish ideas of revelation in the instruction in Gentile Christian churches.

Thesis 7: The relation of the Word to revelation is in terms of prophecy, instruction, and report.[1]

What is significant here is "the accent on the universal historical scope of revelation."[2] There is no cleavage between salvation history and world history; aborted is the idea that from time to time revelation touches history and embroiders it with meaning. Revelation is seen *as* history and not above it or between moments of it. Thus Christianity cannot be established upon pure faith but must be constructed upon reason's appropriation of history. Reason and faith are not antitheses but constitute together the act of a person.

In Pannenberg's Christology we see the definitive form in which his understanding of "revelation as history" is operative. It is not surprising that a theologian would write: "As Christians we know God only as he has been revealed in and through Jesus. . . . One can only speak about God himself in that at the same time one talks about Jesus."[3] That is rather traditional in Christian theology. But then he raises the question of whether Christianity is primarily concerned in Christology with the Jesus of the past or the Jesus who is present. Are we in fact dealing with Jesus or the message of the early Christian community? It has been standard procedure in the years when neo-orthodoxy ruled that the only Jesus we know is the Christ who was proclaimed by faith. We cannot get around the testimony to that which is testified to. Pannenberg argues that "it is quite possible to distinguish the figure of Jesus himself, as well as the outlines of his message, from the particular perspective in which it is transmitted through this or that New Testament witness. . . . Going back behind the apostolic kerygma to the historical Jesus is . . . possible. It is also necessary."[4] Nothing dare be said in faith that does not have support in the historical event of Jesus. It should also be noted that this determination to go behind the records enables us to see "the unity that binds together the New Testament witnesses."[5] Jesus as the historical source of all reports is that in which they hold together.

The task of Christology is to show the revelatory character of the Christ event as something inherent in it and
therefore the basis of faith. In order to do this on terms
Pannenberg contends will constitute public evidence, he
proceeds with a Christology "from below" rather than
a Christology "from above."[6] A Christology "from above"
begins with the divinity of Jesus and accentuates the
incarnation. One starts in the full recognition of who
Jesus really is and proceeds to understand his coming
to a foreign place as the act of God searching for man
in the "far country." Karl Barth is an excellent example
of one who proceeds this way. By contrast, Christology
"from below" moves from the historical man Jesus
toward the recognition of his divinity. From a concern
with his message and fate one comes to realize that
this is an incarnation. Only in this way can we be alert
to the new thing God is doing here and allow him to
define the meaning of the event. "What is inherently
new and contingent in a historical occurrence, and especially in Jesus' history, nevertheless radically qualifies
all foreknowledge, even the foreknowledge about God
that is unavoidably presupposed."[7] Thus we must begin
with the man Jesus not only to be open to the fullness of
the new event, but also to keep our case in public view.

There is, of course, the closest possible relationship
between the questions "who Jesus is" and "who Jesus is
for us." The confession of faith in Jesus belongs together
with his saving significance for us. However true it may
be that we know Jesus in his saving action, his divinity
does not consist in his meaning for us. "The divinity of
Jesus remains the *presupposition* for his saving significance for us and, conversely, the saving significance of
his divinity is the reason why we take *interest* in the

question of his divinity."[8] Here again we see the determination of Pannenberg to argue from evidence and not
to it; he consistently begins in history and not in presuppositions about it. The danger in the alternative is that
one may never in fact talk about Jesus at all but only
assumptions about him. Pannenberg is clearly a ration-
alist in that he is not prepared to accept anything beyond
what is yielded by the evidence.

The central thrust of his theology of history is evident
in his treatment of the resurrection of Jesus. Pannenberg
is anxious that we not assert as theologically true what
has no historical truth. There is no justification in arguing
from the claims Jesus makes for his unity with God and
therefore to the viability of the resurrection. We will have
to examine the resurrection event to see if it establishes
the unity of Jesus with God. Jesus' claims await confirma-
tion by God in the resurrection. Pannenberg is prepared
and eager to have the revelation of God in Christ hinge
on the resurrection as an event in history and not in the
consciousness of the disciples.

It is tempting to focus our questions about the resurrection on its meaning and on the plausibility of belief in
it today. Pannenberg meets these questions[9] head on, but
they are not directly relevant to us now. What is necessary for us is to face the issue of history: Did something
happen? Was it something for which at that time there
was public evidence? Is there at least a kernel of history
to the stories? His answer to these queries is affirmative,
but what is significant is the way he arrives at that
conclusion.

Without embarrassment Pannenberg acknowledges that
we are dealing with a metaphor. "To speak about the
resurrection of the dead is not comparable to speaking

about any random circumstance that can be identified
empirically at any time."[10] It is of the nature of metaphor
that it combines what we know in experience with what
cannot be experienced at least for now. The claim is made
that as one is awakened from sleep and rises, so the dead
will be raised. We can only experience in our common
life the phenomenon of being awakened, but this enables
us to throw this experience against one that is beyond
us. What faith does is project this-worldly images against
occurrences that are beyond this world.

Having granted the metaphorical character of the language, one needs to remember what the historian brings
to the consideration at hand. If he has decided that resurrection of the dead is not a possibility, then there is little
or no likelihood he will find convincing evidence. However, one can begin with the assumption that it is possible
and therefore be open to its truth. It is this latter posture
which Pannenberg assumes for reasons that are common
to human expectations of existence and to late Jewish
apocalypticism. Furthermore, contemporary science frees
us of the deterministic world view of previous genera-
tions and enables us to assume a genuinely open future.
Granted this possibility, he notes that we are dealing
with two different traditions which must be evaluated
separately. One is the appearances of the resurrected one
and the other is the empty tomb. We will only consider
the appearances.

Pannenberg makes swift work of the appearances reported in the Gospels, contending that they have a
"strongly legendary character."[11] However, the testimony
of the Pauline report, I Cor. 15:1–11, is clearly an attempt
"to give proof by means of witnesses for the facticity of
Jesus' resurrection."[12] Verse 6 claims that the appear-

ance was to more than five hundred, many of whom are still alive at the time of writing. Obviously this is a report by one near to the event and with others alive who can corroborate it. In addition he uses a clearly formulated tradition to state his case; it is not Paul's *ad hoc* memory but something carefully worked out and in circulation. We are dealing then with appearances that are clearly attested by the apostles. Now Pannenberg claims that the resurrection can be called a historical event in this sense: "If the emergence of primitive Christianity, which, apart from other traditions, is also traced back by Paul to appearances of the resurrected Jesus, can be understood in spite of all critical examination of the tradition only if one examines it in the light of the eschatological hope for a resurrection from the dead, then that which is so designated is a historical event, even if we do not know anything more particular about it. Then an event that is expressible only in the language of the eschatological expectation is to be asserted as a historical occurrence."[13] Another way of stating this is to say that the case against the factuality of the resurrection would have to be made by showing that some other kind of event occurred that can make better sense of the texts.

This discussion of the resurrection reveals how seriously Pannenberg takes the matter of history and how dependent faith is upon its results. It is only in a historical resurrection that the divinity of Jesus can be recognized and that God's revelation takes place. This is the argument "from below" in that one comes to conclusions from history rather than brings presuppositions to it. This is also subjecting the faith to public evidence. The resurrection confirms the unity of God with Christ and there revelation occurs as history. This rather lengthy treatment is relevant to our study as it points up that the reality of God can only be established on historical terms. We can anchor our beliefs and our hopes in events and not be intimidated by their provisionality. If a case cannot be made from public evidence, then there is no basis for Christian claims. History must justify faith. Not in recent times has a theologian, apart from the literalists, made such bold claims for history as revelation.

Against this background we can speak more specifically of Pannenberg's doctrine of God. He proceeds to this through consideration of the Kingdom of God whose imminence is central in Jesus' teachings. In recent years discussion of this has been impeded by confusing the Kingdom as the sphere of obedience to God with the notion that it is something men establish and extend. Pannenberg contends that this is a distortion of Jesus' proclamation. The Kingdom is something that is announced, setting everything in the present under its imminent power. "This future is expected to come in a marvelous way from God himself; it is not simply the development of human history or the achievement of God-fearing men."[14] His understanding of the Kingdom is eschatological rather than ethical. It is the coming and present rule of God rather than the creation of man's goodness.

Futurity is an essential concept for understanding the eschatological situation that God is bringing about. But it is crucial to recognize that "God's rule is not simply in the future, leaving men to do nothing but wait quietly for its arrival."[15] It is a characteristic of Jesus' proclamation of the Kingdom that future and present are not separable. "Jesus underscored the *present impact* of the imminent future."[16] It does violence to Jesus' message when we abstract either the future from the present or the present from the future in his message. While futurity is fundamental, it has interwoven with it the impact upon the present. Jesus modified the hope of the Jewish community to the extent that he proclaimed the Kingdom as imminent and not something totally ahead of us. Indeed, the future makes a claim upon the present; men are called to align their priorities in the light of the urgency created by the coming Kingdom. Rather than argue that the future is a result of the past and the present, Jesus sees the future as determining the present and the past. The idea of God is, of course, to be interpreted in this context even though the raw materials for this in Jesus' teachings are rather scant.

The anticipated rule of God enables us to understand his being and existence. Philosophically we can say that "the being of the gods is their power."[17] If a man affirms one god, he believes that one power dominates everything. It is intrinsic to the nature of God to have power over finite creation. "The deity of God is his rule."[18] In Jesus' proclamation this rule belongs to the future; he preaches a coming Kingdom. To this traditional Jewish understanding Jesus added the conviction that the claim God had upon the world could only be viewed from the perspective of its coming and not its actuality. In a restricted sense one can say that "God does not yet exist. Since his rule and his being are inseparable, God's being is still in the process of coming to be."[19] In other words, the association of being and rule means that God is not known now in the fullness of his reality but that is to come at the end. The reality of God is ahead of us and not to be expected in the midst of us. Obviously this invites comparison with Schubert Ogden. Pannenberg acknowledges certain similarities between this thought and that of Whitehead upon whom Ogden draws heavily. The difference, perhaps, is in terms of emphasis. While

Ogden lays stress upon becoming, Pannenberg concentrates upon futurity. In the one we have the sense of "moving toward" the future and in the other the future "reaching back" to the present. For Pannenberg, God will only be revealed fully at the end; for Ogden he is being created in his being along the way.

If we read God in terms of his coming rule, then he is to be understood as the power of the future that determines everything that is present. This idea of God deduced from the imminence of the Kingdom in Jesus' message has viability for contemporary man in his struggle to understand reality. "By conceiving of God as the power of the future, the word 'God' acquires a new concreteness."[20] The world is then understood as a consequence of the power of the future which has been labeled "God." It is not too difficult for us to understand the future as not imprisoned by the past and present. In our actual relationship to the future we know it both as a threatening power and as the possibility of fulfillment independent of what has gone before. There is also a degree of indeterminateness in nature. Neither nature nor history is entirely predictable from the past or present conditions that prevail. There is an element of contingency by which Pannenberg means that "something is decided that was only a possibility before."[21] In other words, the contingency of events in nature and history means that they are not completely determined but the future is in fact open to occurrences that are not results of previous causes. There is an unboundedness and unexpectedness to our experience. Traditionally God is perceived as bearing a relationship to this contingency in nature and history. But while we may be able to imagine that these contingencies are under the power of the future, how can we say it is God whom we encounter in these events? Are we justified in claiming them as acts of God? This much can be said with confidence: "The contingency of events is a crucial presupposition for understanding the future as personal, and to speak of God is to speak of a personal power."[22]

Pannenberg recognizes that to speak of God as personal is to invite the charge of projection. Man experiences himself as personal and he projects a superimage of himself upon reality. But this is arbitrary and artificial in that it is a development of recent history and cannot be traced back where it should have been operative if it were true. From anthropology we find no evidence of it in preliterate or archaic man. He understood himself in terms of the gods and not the other way around. "Weighty evidence favors the idea of the personal having its origins in religious experience, in the encounter with divine reality."[23] The idea of the person was transposed from the gods to man and not from man to the gods. In any case contingent events were conceived as personal acts.

Yet contingency must be coupled with "a unity behind contingent self-expressions"[24] to certify their personal quality. Meaningful connections between events is the nature of unity even though the element of contingency is in force as well. Unity implies continuity and coherence. And Pannenberg sees this as springing from the future. "In every event the infinite future separates itself from the finite events which until then had been hidden in this future but are now released into existence. The future lets go of itself to bring into being our present."[25] When in the present we are confronted by this infinite future and welcome the events that are released from it, "we anticipate the coming of God."[26] Pannenberg in this argument is, of course, assuming that there is a common future toward which all events move. The connections we experience between events in our lives suggest to us the future as a unifying power. When man asks after the ultimate unity that draws everything together, he is forming the question of God. The burden of this argument on unity and contingency has been to demonstrate that there is a base in existential awareness for the affirmation of faith. It is to this that Pannenberg can now say: "God in his very being is the future of the world. All experience of the future is, at least indirectly, related to God himself. In this case every event in which the future becomes finitely present must be understood as a contingent act of God, who places that finite reality into being by distinguishing it from his own powerful future."[27] This is the implication drawn from Jesus' message of the imminent Kingdom of God.

It might be suspected that a theology which places such emphasis upon the future has in fact banished God to some distant point. But this is not the case with Pannenberg's treatment. It is precisely in the futurity of God that he dominates the past as well as the present. "The God of the coming Kingdom must be called eternal because he is not only the future of our present but has been also the future of every past age."[28] To each present in its own time God has assigned a future which now has simply become past for us. The futurity of God is thus operative in even the remotest past. There is nothing, including the nothingness before creation, of which God is not the future. While it cannot in the present be known in a definitive sense that God exists, it will be known in the future as what was true all along. This again is what differentiates Pannenberg from Whitehead and Ogden. The priority Pannenberg gives the future does not mean God will be something different at the end than he was in the past. However, Pannenberg is not saying that God is future only from the standpoint of how he appears to us; he is the power of the future in himself. There is no future beyond him; "he is the ultimate future."[29] Nothing can surpass it.

In summary, we have seen that for Pannenberg the Kingdom of God is the heart of Jesus' proclamation. This means that men always live in the time when the future is about to happen and is in fact reaching into the present. There is purposeful intent in history in that the power of the future is present leading it to what will one day be its fullness. This alone enables all events in all times to cohere. The coming Kingdom impinges upon every now and determines its meaning and destiny. From this understanding of the Kingdom we have at least embryonically a concept of God as the power of the future. This, of course, is not a future with a blank face. In the historical event of Jesus and his resurrection we get a view of what is to come. We can expect it to be defined by love. The reality of God is established by Pannenberg in two ways. First, it must be historical and open to public view. Rational man must be able to determine the viability of faith from the evidence history affords. We saw this illustrated particularly in the resurrection of Jesus. Secondly, the reality of God is experienced in man's existential awareness of the future. This gives evidence that our lives are "related to an abundant future which transcends all finite happenings."[30] The ultimate power locked in the future which unites everything is called God.

One of the most substantial contributions of Pannenberg's has to do with restoring the significance of history. He saves it not only from the naturalism and positivism of the nineteenth century but also from the existentialist and "Word of God" dissipation of it in the twentieth. Pannenberg draws us back to the realization that Christianity as a historical religion must be willing to deal with that history. Those who, for example, affirmed the Christ of faith but were embarrassed by what we know about Jesus of Nazareth surely were unfaithful to the nature of the New Testament records. There is a distinct relationship between the credibility of faith and the accessibility of history to support it. With his interpretation of revelation as history, Pannenberg makes an effort to bring Christian faith into the court of public evidence. And then, in bringing every aspect of life under the impact of the coming Kingdom, Pannenberg has proposed a doctrine of God that embraces the social conditions of men. It draws our attention beyond the individual to the historical communities of which he is a part. The posture of the lonely individual related to God through his guilt, anxiety, and meaninglessness in existentialism has lost persuasiveness. Our problems now are more societal than individual. In many instances we find that there is little, if any, connection between a man's theology and his social concerns. Pannenberg has corrected that in his own theology: "The understanding of social change is clearly and inextricably connected to the doctrine of God, for everything that has been said about the power of the future is in fact about the nature of God."[31] One could not relate the two much more intimately without losing the identity of the one or the other.

For all the boldness and originality of Pannenberg's work, reservations have been registered against it at several points. Helmut Gollwitzer, professor of systematic theology at the Free University of Berlin, argues that Pannenberg is ambiguous when he attempts to utilize facts in constituting public evidence for faith. "Pannenberg . . . takes back with the one hand what he gives with the other, when he says on the one hand that for the knowledge of God 'the language of facts' is sufficient, . . . without it being necessary to add anything that would allow us to see in the events 'anything other than what can be found in them themselves'—but on the other hand he makes the reservation that the 'revealing facts' 'are naturally not to be regarded as brute facts, but in their context in the history of tradition.'"[32] It would seem that one could not have it both ways. If Pannenberg really proposes to establish faith on historical grounds and anchor the knowledge of God in the fact of the risen Christ, then in a very real sense these facts should speak for themselves. Nothing indeed need be added for them to be convincing to those who will look at the events without preconceptions. Yet apparently Pannenberg is not convinced that brute facts are sufficiently persuasive. A history of tradition is required in order for their meaning to be "indubitably certain." While it is not necessary for us to bring faith with us to grasp the knowledge of God revealed in history, it is necessary to have a context in which "uninhibited observation" can take place. Gollwitzer's point is that Pannenberg is in a very ambiguous position when he talks about the "language of facts" speaking on behalf of their own meaning. It appears he does not trust them in the courts of public evidence as radically as he first implies; they must be appropriated in the "context of the history of tradition."

Obviously what Pannenberg is striving to avoid is the disposition of a Bultmann to dismiss facts on behalf of the kerygma, to ignore the facticity of history in favor of the meaning of historical events to witnesses. But in the process he has gone to the extreme of affirming the objectivity of the happenedness of revelation in order to avoid the existential subjectivity of his predecessors. Carl E. Braaten contends that Pannenberg's confidence in the facts of history and a tradition saturated with their meaning causes him to distort the nature and place of the kerygma. If revelation comes to us in "the language of facts," certainly this diminishes "the indispensable place of the kerygma as the mediator of the knowledge of historical revelation."[33] The transmission of the meaning of events "from faith to faith" is a process for which Pannenberg leaves little room. The New Testament record is more than facts and a tradition that delivers their meaning. It is, argues Braaten, a document that holds up as well the response of faith to saving events. If we take seriously the New Testament, we have to be responsible to the claim that faith comes through preaching, the proclamation of the meaning of historical events. Fearing subjectivity, Pannenberg understates the function of the kerygma and the Spirit in delivery of God's revelation and in bringing man to faith; he overstates the capacity of reason and historical fact to be lucid and persuasive.

Perhaps a more serious issue raised with Pannenberg comes from John B. Cobb, Jr., Ingraham Professor of Theology at the School of Theology at Claremont, California. In a substantial article in reaction to *Jesus—God and Man,* Cobb acknowledges that "this book is virtually alone in working out precise, fresh solutions of traditional issues in detailed interaction with the whole history of Christian thought."[34] Yet Cobb challenges Pannenberg for the way in which he makes the reality of God in Christ rest upon the facticity of the resurrection. For Pannenberg, Jesus as the resurrected one is God proleptically; he is the source of vision into the nature of God at the end. What is real only in the future has a point of historical disclosure in the event of the resurrection.

But Cobb asks if the support for the facticity of the resurrection is persuasive. "Even if we allow the *possibility* of unique events in the past, quite discontinuous with our ordinary experience, should we not require considerably more evidence for their occurrence than for that of ordinary events?"[35] Can the appearances of Jesus as they are attested by witnesses really be persuasive in supporting what God will come to mean? Do they give an advance vision of the reality of God? It would seem that to tie the credibility of God this decisively to an event in history would require more support than the New Testament affords. Faith may indeed be futile if Christ is not raised, but the historicity of Jesus' rising from the dead may not be the place at which one wants to rest the case for faith. Cobb is arguing at least implicitly that Pannenberg has provided here a linchpin that may be removed without too much strain and in the process cripple our access to the reality of God. While retreating into a faith assertion may not be viable at this point, it would seem that public evidence for the unity of God and Christ revealed in the resurrection is not the most solid ground upon which to stand either. It is one thing to affirm that the resurrection establishes the deity of Jesus and another to have the historicity of this determine the credibility of God. For the revelation of God in Christ to rest upon the resurrection as a historically verifiable event may be entirely too vulnerable a base.

These reservations notwithstanding, Pannenberg has made a stunning contribution to the issue of the reality of God in our lived experience by introducing the dimension of future. God as the power of the future impinging upon and determining the present is persuasive and suggestive for many who want to understand God in relation to the dynamics of our time.

7

JÜRGEN MOLTMANN
God as the Promise of a New Future

IN THE FORMATION OF HIS THEOLOGY every theologian makes a decision about his age. He may decide, as in the case of Karl Barth, that the interpretation of the faith must be protected from influence by the culture in which he lives. More likely, he will select a discipline or a disposition he feels dominates the culture and interpret the faith through it or at least in relation to it. Dietrich Bonhoeffer recognized the disposition to secularization and programmed his theological task in response to it. Paul M. van Buren detected the empirical temper of his time and allowed linguistic analysis to determine the boundaries of theological discourse. Jürgen Moltmann has made a decision in favor of the principle of hope as it is expressed in the writings of a Jewish-Marxist-atheist, Ernst Bloch. Moltmann writes: "As scarcely any other philosophy [Bloch's] *Das Prinzip Hoffnung* (*The Principle of Hope*) is suited to help in activating and elaborating the Christian doctrine of hope. . . . [It] can in the present situation of Christian theology give us courage to try a new interpretation of the original Christian hope."[1] This, parenthetically, is a judgment in which Wolfhart Pannenberg concurs. Bloch has led Pannenberg to the category of the future as central but enters less rigorously into dialogue with Bloch than Moltmann. The decision about one's age is always fraught with ambiguity. If one does not tie into it at some decisive point, he risks being totally irrelevant in his theology; when he does tie into it, he risks distorting the faith by this very commitment. Moltmann protects himself more skillfully than most in that he repudiates the temptation to take over a secular form of hope. Rather, he contends that Bloch directs Christians to the nature of the hope inherent in the Biblical witness.

When Moltmann wrestles with the question, Where in our lived experience does God become real? he directs us into the heart of Biblical eschatology. God is known to us in his promises for a qualitatively new future; the future is the mode of his being with us. His faithfulness to promises in the past is the beginning of our understanding of God. This note of futurity in the Christian tradition corresponds to the most real aspect of our lived experience: man everywhere is asking for something distinctively new. God is he who is coming in the future as a new event.

Granted his decision on behalf of the principle of hope and its function within theology, we need briefly to examine what Moltmann is resonating with in Bloch. Bloch affirms that the nature of existence in particular and reality in general is movement toward the future. The experience of the "not yetness" of it all, in which the limitations we experience in the present are overcome, is the central category for understanding. Life proceeds from an unfinished past toward a future that is not fully determined; it is experienced as latency for something. Man knows himself as on the way to a future; this is the nature of things both for humanity and in nature. That toward which humanity is on the way is a "homeland," a utopian condition that will never occur but will always be present as a possibility. The future is a direction not a destination for Bloch; it is not something at which one arrives but toward which one always moves. Existence moves forward toward the new that overcomes present conditions. Hope is the core of existence, the very substance of reality. Yet for Bloch there is no transcendent guarantee of fulfillment.

This brings us to the intriguing analysis Bloch makes of religion. The philosopher argues that the real substratum built into all religions is hope. Religion and hope are intrinsically related; wherever one finds the latter he will find the former. Religion is to the very core futuristic. Often this has meant that it distorted hope by holding out vain promises and enabled persons to escape the present. But in its most authentic forms religion is a reservoir of forces for hope which has left its mark on history. The estate willed to mankind in religion is eschatological hope. "According to Bloch, the longing that gives rise to religion, the desire of oppressed creation for joy, for happiness, and for hope, has its roots in 'that dichotomy in man which is so pregnant wih religion— the dichotomy between his present appearance and his non-present essence.' "[2] This is the ontic foundation from which religion arises. Religion is rooted in the process character of man and his world, in the inevitable surge from what is to what is not yet. The core of reality in man and the cosmos is a mainstring drawn taut toward what will be.

But what can God mean in this for Bloch? In one sense, Bloch is saying that God is shorthand for man. The word can stand for the unfulfilled humanity beyond which man presses. He is an image for the undiscovered future humanity, the unknown man who is "not yet." " 'God' is understood as a 'utopian hypostatization of the ideal of the unknown man.' "[3] By the gods, men express their movement toward the longed-for future. Yet in another sense, Bloch does not want us to deal with gods as if they were real in themselves. The idea of God as perfect or as a fulfilled reality is an anathema to Bloch. He is an atheist. When one affirms a God in the usual sense this means that the future is already determined and therefore not really open. The way things are going to turn out is already decided and this is the antithesis of true hope in the "not-yet." Bloch contends that the Bible itself is affirming "movement toward" rather than "arrival at" as the nature of its hope. Its central categories are a coming Kingdom, the exodus, a new heaven and a new earth. These do not imply that reality is closed but that it is open endlessly and everlastingly toward the future. Bloch even goes so far as to suggest that a good Christian must be an atheist. There is no transcendent reality in Biblical eschatology according to Bloch; there is transcending hope for the future. The accounts are not settled in advance but remain open forever. There remain infinite possibilities. One does not need the reality of God to thrust man forward toward the future; in fact, that holds back his impulses. That which is the source of the drive toward the future is matter. It is the ground of possibility. The longing of matter for form is that in which the principle of hope adheres.

Moltmann does not react uncritically to the philosophy of hope as expounded by Bloch.[4] For our purposes, however, enough has been said to create an impression of what Moltmann affirms as the central motif in culture

which enables us to understand Biblical eschatology. This
doctrine has been either distorted or lost in recent theological trends. It has been interpreted in such a way as
to postpone everything of significance to the end time or
to dissipate the end time in favor of an urgent present.
It has been made peripheral either to the gospel or to the
immediate concerns of men. It has been anything but at
the center in any authentic way. Moltmann, under the
impact of Bloch, contends that "Christianity is eschatology, is hope, forward looking and forward moving, and
therefore also revolutionizing and transforming the present."[5] We are not to understand it as one of Christianity's
constituent parts but that which constitutes its very existence. The problem of the future is *the* problem of Christian theology. Proper theology begins with the end!
Christianity does not just speak of any future but of a
definitive moment in history through which the reality of
the future is understood. It is concerned with "Jesus
Christ and *his* future."[6] The utopianism of Bloch and
others is differentiated from eschatology in the Christian
sense precisely because "all statements about the future
are grounded in the person and history of Jesus Christ."[7]
Because of the resurrection of the Crucified One, Christians live by promises in a hidden future which yet influences the present in which it announces the end. These
promises contradict the prevailing conditions of men and
thus can only be experienced as negation of what is. The
promise of that which is new does not just throw light
on the present but creates the possibility of what is to be.
The future has to do with transformation not information.
The New Testament message is a "hoping against hope,"
a living on behalf of what will be even though the present
does not support it. It is hope in spite of the future pros-

pects one might expect on the basis of experience. The Christian strains after the future because of the promises of God for it in Jesus Christ. "Those who hope in Christ can no longer put up with reality as it is, but begin to suffer under it, to contradict it. . . . The goad of the promised future stabs inexorably into the flesh of every unfulfilled present."[8] Sin is the failure to hope and act upon the promises.

Inevitably we wonder about the connection between the hope of natural man and the hope of the Christian man in the promises of God. How are they related? Moltmann argues on two levels. First, the hope of faith has a critical role in relation to the human movements of hope. It opposes "the vain glory in every movement filled with human hope"; it exposes "their uncritical naivete."[9] In the name of its own "better promises" it exposes those utopian visions which cannot accomplish man's reconciliation with his existence but cheat him into believing that things are getting better. The hope of faith has the task of "destroying the infection of presumption and of resignation" which is the disease of human hopes. True hope purges false hopes. Yet secondly, the hope of faith has a positive role. It can become "a source of creative and inventive imagination in the service of love, and must release anticipatory thought that asks about the present possibility of man's life here becoming better, more just, freer, and more humane."[10] True hope in the promises of God is alert to the instances of emerging possibilities in history and takes them up into the Christian hope. It seeks out in the present what is opening up to the future and which bears some correspondence to the future as promised by God. The hope of faith makes common cause where it can with lesser hopes to the end that they be brought into a fulfillment not within their reach. It is willing and eager to direct what is already going to what is beyond the possibilities of the present.

It is essential to grasp Moltmann's understanding of revelation. Revelation is not to be understood first in relation to the doctrine of God, the Word of God, or man's self-understanding; it must be understood eschatologically. The promises of God for the future are the locus of revelation of God. "Faith is called to life by promise and is therefore essentially hope, confidence, trust in the God who will not lie but will remain faithful to his promise."[11] The central cradle and matrix for the promise are the Easter appearances. On the one hand, these appearances are the occasion for recognizing Jesus as he really *was*. This is faith's historical mooring. But on the other hand, Easter also concerns the "not yet apparent future of the risen Lord."[12] These appearances are the occasion for the recognition of what Jesus really *will be*. There is as yet an outstanding future; there is the promise of a reality not yet existing. Thus Moltmann's understanding of the promises does not merely illuminate something inherent in reality but the anticipation of something new which we have no right to expect on other terms. The stage of history is thrown open. There is an expectation of a "creative act."

In contrast to this eschatological understanding of revelation as the promise of God is the loss of a real future in Barth's and Bultmann's views of eschatology. For Barth revelation is the coming of the Eternal to man. What God reveals is himself; revelation is the self-disclosure of God. It is the sharing of what God knows about himself. In this context God proves himself to man. He reveals himself as he is "beforehand in himself."

But this "is to take the question as to the future and the goal indicated by revelation, and answer it with a reflection on the origin of revelation, on God himself. With this reflection, however, it becomes almost impossible to see the revelation of the risen Lord as the ground for still speaking of an outstanding future of Jesus Christ."[13] Barth's view does not open up the future in terms of promise. Bultmann flattens out eschatology in a similar way. Revelation has to do with man and his coming into his authentic selfhood. All statements about God and his activity are interpreted in terms of their connection with our existence. While the question of God is raised within the question of existence, what is finally disclosed to man is his real selfhood. Thus the goal or future of God is man's realization of his true being. But in the process "eschatology has wholly lost its sense as goal of history, and is in fact understood as the goals of the individual human being."[14] In revelation man is opened up to himself, but there is beyond that no opening up of history to a new possibility. Bultmann, like Barth, has really taken the future out of eschatology. According to Moltmann, they preach a "God without future" and mesh unwittingly with a culture that preaches a "future without God."

Now if revelation is understood eschatologically, how does God become knowable? First, God reveals himself by his faithfulness to his promises in history. He can be recognized where in his acts of faithfulness he makes good on the promises he has made. "Where God, in his faithfulness to a promise he has given, stands to that which he has promised to be, he becomes manifest and knowable as the selfsame Self."[15] It is in the constancy and correspondence of promise and action that God be-

comes known. This is to say that we know what we are
looking for in the promises of God and we know him
really when he evidences in history his faithfulness. The
knowledge of God is a matter of re-cognition. Only God
can confess to God and he confirms himself to man by
making good on what he has promised to do.

Secondly, the knowledge of God is always a knowledge
that we ourselves have been called into history by God.
Man is drawn up into that which is yet to be fulfilled.
"God is not first known at the end of history, but in the
midst of history while it is in the making, remains open
and depends on the play of the promises."[16] It is not
merely what has gone on that elicits faith from man but
what is going on in fulfillments yet to be. When we concern ourselves with knowing God we are caught up in
accounts that are not yet closed but are outstanding.
Knowledge is thus concerned with the "outlooks" pred-
icated on past promises and faithfulness. In this sense it
is anticipatory. The promises are dynamic words that
point us beyond completed facts to a future that contra-
dicts reality as we now experience it.

Thirdly, the knowledge of God in his promises for the
future in history involves us in an experience of tension.
We know ourselves to be between something that has
been issued and something that is yet to come to pass.
Man is bound by the strain toward what is coming. In
this sense it can be said that his hope is not in God as
such but that the future will bear the marks of his faithfulness. Man in the interval experiences birth pangs as
the promises press against him. "The God who is present
in his promises is for the human spirit an object . . . in
the sense that he stands opposed to . . . the human spirit
until a reality is created and becomes knowable which

wholly accords with his promises and can be called 'very good.'"[17] Man is driven beyond himself and in the experience of transcendence is called to obedience. Man must arise and go in freedom toward the fulfillment of promises. In this sense he must keep the promises himself. But to do this is to live in an "interval of tension." The knowledge of God is the knowledge that we are pulled into the future ourselves and out of the security of encapsulation.

Now that we have some understanding of how God becomes known for Moltmann, we must proceed to examine more carefully the nature of what is known. It should not surprise us that the God of promises should be interpreted as the creator of a qualitatively new future. God is he who is doing and will do a new thing. In the Old Testament we find Yahweh understood not only as the One who had been faithful to Israel in the exodus but as a God who was heralded as about to do a new act. "A new future is to come from God, a future new and unexpected."[18] The prophets speak of it in terms of a "new David," a "new covenant," and a "new exodus." Thus they link the new reality God will create with his faithfulness in the past. When one turns to the New Testament one finds in Paul an even more radical expectancy. "The new is not a mere renewal, but the entrance of the unexpected."[19] The new event of the future is not understood in terms of past events and traditions. "The old has passed away, behold, the new has come." (II Cor. 5:17.) This is not a continuation of the best in the past or present but a totally new thing. It is not linked with what man can do (as in Ernst Bloch's philosophy) but the faithfulness of God to his promises now and always. Moltmann thus understands God as he who "creates a qualitatively new future."[20]

We can grasp this fully only through the resurrection of Jesus. "The all-embracing vision of God and of the new creation is for Christian hope anchored in the resurrection of the crucified Christ."[21] There one gets a glimmer of the "power of the new world." In Jesus the future has begun even as it is yet to be. The apostles understood this resurrection as the dawning, the expectation, and the representation of a future beyond normal anticipations. The Easter event has a historical framework but is not itself historically verifiable. It is not a universally visible drama as yet. Only the cross as a sign of hope can be directly verified; it is the "present form of the resurrection"[22] and as such the ground of hope. Yet it is the resurrection per se that is the sign of the future. Through it God is understood as the power of the new. Granted the crucifixion, it is a creation out of nothingness. The cross represents God-forsakenness and hell; but precisely these conditions are overcome with the resurrection. And this is the basis for the confidence that man will be given a new future in which death, pain, weeping, evil, and guilt will be conquered. Through the resurrection "the promise of a future which stands against frustration, transiency, and death"[23] is assured for faith. This is a state that has not existed before and reflects the God who creates a "qualitatively new future" for mankind.

Now we need to be clear that for Moltmann we are not dealing with a "future-future" but a "present-future." The God whom we know as the power of the future and from whom we expect a new thing reaches back into the present. Indeed, the future is God's mode of being with us. He is with man as he who is coming. In this sense the future qualifies the present. With the carrying out of his reign now he is the coming Lord. Moltmann argues that we should not think of "God above us" or "God between us" but "God in front of us, ahead of us." The God of the exodus is the one who leads us out of the present into an unknown future with only the assurance that he is the future before us. As the coming God he liberates us from the securities of the present and the shackles of the past for the possibilities of the future. The future as his mode of being with us means that "his future takes control over the present in real anticipations and prefigurations."[24] However, this does not mean that his "eternal presence" is with us. Because he is the power of the future, there is a "not yet" quality to his presence. "The dialectic between his being and his being-not-yet is the pain and the power of history. Caught between the experience of his presence and of his absence, we are seeking his future."[25] The interval in which we live is drawn ahead by the God who is before us; he who creates a new possibility draws us into the process through which the new is coming.

This necessitates our giving brief consideration to what Moltmann means by political theology. Politics here does not mean joining a party, though it might include that. Rather, Moltmann uses the term as a reference to those forms of human association and the utilization of power in society which either foster or impede the realization of human possibilities. To be political in one's theology is to put oneself between the promises of God and the actualities of historical experience. It is in the arena of political action that the quality of human life is being determined and not in some mysterious soul of the individual. Indeed, the modern critics of religion are no longer asking about its philosophical truth but about its relation to social and economic structures and the contribution it makes to the humanizing processes in our soci-

ety. Does it sanction systems that lead to the fulfillment
of human possibilities or does it sanction those which
cripple men? Does it align itself with movements of liberation or does it join forces of human repression? The
function of political theology is to make men aware of
the dimension of the human amid the processes of the
social order. Righteousness must be sought on the streets
and not in the soul. Faith is not to be understood as a
dialogue between good men about spiritual matters but
as action in the world under the promises of God. Of
course, this does not mean the identification of God or
the gospel with any particular movement and lending it
sanctity. But it does mean aligning oneself with the risks
for humanization of society, speaking the right words in
the right places, doing the right thing at the right time.
Political theology is involved and practical. In this sense
it follows the Crucified One whom Moltmann contends
offended the political empire at its nerve center and therefore was "tried" as an enemy of the state. To wait for the
promises of God to be fulfilled in a new future is to
participate politically toward the intentions of God for
mankind. Man is saved in the political arena; there he
may be crucified as well. But he will have spoken politically of God with his life. And he will have sought the
righteousness of God in the world where it is to be found.

In that they are radically oriented toward the future,
Pannenberg and Moltmann have much in common. Both
interpret God as the power of the future, accentuate the
place of history in theology, and perceive the resurrection of Jesus as an anticipation of the end of history. Lest
the impression be created that the one is a carbon copy
of the other, however, we need to indicate very briefly
where their theologies diverge. When Pannenberg was

asked at the International Theological Seminar in Munich, June, 1969, where he and Moltmann differed he said: "Moltmann, under the influence of Karl Barth, still works from the 'word of God' and that is an essentially mythological starting point. I begin with revelation as history." This would seem to be confirmed in our study by the emphasis we have seen that Moltmann puts on the "promises of God" and the emphasis Pannenberg puts on the facticity of the resurrection. They also differ in subtle but significant ways on matters pertaining to the resurrection. Moltmann is uncomfortable with Pannenberg's claim that the resurrection is the expected end of history. This is to imply that Jesus has no future beyond that which he has already attained. The risen Christ has no future and Christians cannot then look forward to a new event in the future. Their expectation can only be that what happened to Jesus will happen to them. The two theologians also differ in that Moltmann draws the cross more radically into his interpretation of the resurrection. "Jesus' resurrection may have been understood as a *sign* of hope for a God-forsaken mankind. But only his cross was the real mediation of this hope for the hopeless. Thus the cross is the present form of the resurrection."[26] In addition, while Pannenberg most frequently refers to Jesus as the risen Lord, Moltmann most frequently refers to him as the Crucified One. Finally, we find that Moltman is a thoroughly dialectical thinker. He affirms that novelty emerges from contradiction. We have seen evidence of this method at several points but most recently in the claim that God backs up against man and the present conditions he endures until he creates a reality that accords with his promises. There is nothing comparable in Pannenberg to this dialectical process. For all the similarities between the two, they each have a separate and identifiable program.

The contribution of Moltmann to our understanding of God in lived experience drives beyond that of Pannenberg's at essentially one point: God is not only the power of the future but the promise of a qualitatively new future. In speaking about the future of the risen Christ and thus marking the true openness of the future, Moltmann would seem to do justice to the New Testament expectation that God will yet do a new thing. He senses the claim that something significantly new is coming, not that something previously accomplished is about to be revealed. The importance of this is that it protects the freedom of God. There is no reason to limit him to the fulfillment of a past accomplishment on a wider scale. If God is God, then he can bring about a future event that is qualitatively not just quantitatively new.

One of the questions that inevitably is raised about a theologian like Moltmann centers on the decision he makes about his age. It must be acknowledged that in some form and in some degree this is both inevitable and necessary. Yet problems immediately emerge and Peter Berger, professor of sociology at the New School for Social Research, has been perceptive in identifying two of them. While he does not mention Moltmann, it is the kind of accommodation he makes to Ernst Bloch and the spirit of the age that Berger has in mind. One of the problems is holding intact the distinctive contribution of religion once you have granted that a secular philosopher is saying some of the same things as the theologian. Berger's contention is that it requires "considerable exertion to demonstrate that the religious label, as modified in conformity with the spirit of the age, has

anything special to offer."[27] Specifically, why not stay
with Ernst Bloch and his understanding of hope? Is there
anything added by going into Biblical eschatology? Obviously from the perspective of Moltmann much is added;
the question becomes, How persuasive can he be once he
has begun on someone else's terms? While theological
integrity is maintained by moving through Moltmann's
analysis of the promises of God as they are anticipated
in the resurrection of Jesus, it must be recognized that
Bloch's analysis of Biblical eschatology without God has
its own integrity. When Christianity enters the picture
as "that something more" it is in an awkward position.
Those who build on the constructs of secular thought
often create the effect of having spoiled the original archi-
tecture by adding on something. In defense of Moltmann
it must be said that his intent is to use Bloch as a wedge
into Biblical eschatology and not as a superstructure upon
which to build.

Berger's second point is an extension of the first. When
a theologian like Moltmann takes a secular philosopher
with radical seriousness he risks making more accom-
modations than he may be aware of. "In other words,
once one starts a process of cognitive bargaining, one
subjects oneself to mutual cognitive contamination. . . .
The theologian who trades ideas with the modern world,
therefore, is likely to come out with a poor bargain, that
is, he will probably have to give far more than he will
get."[28] For Moltmann to read the spirit of the age through
Bloch may limit his responsiveness to understandings of
the age in the Biblical witness. In taking cues from the
culture, a theologian may miss those defined by the gospel. It must be said again that Moltmann with his emphasis upon the Biblical tradition makes an exceptional effort

to protect himself on this count. Perhaps it would be fairer to say that Berger's two points should be pressed against Moltmann more as a word of caution than of criticism.

When Moltmann operates on the premise that "reality is altogether historical," he evokes a significant criticism from Hans W. Frei, of Yale's Department of Religious Studies. Frei is so bold as to label this "nonsense"; "far from being modern, it is, as a wholesale claim, completely anachronistic. This is not to deny its significance as a partial perspective, or as one of a number of possible world views or conceptual schemes—but no more than that."[29] The basic issue is not what Moltmann does but what he does not do. Having committed himself radically to the premise about history, he provides no point of contact with other dimensions of modern man's experience. Specifically, Moltmann does not give us a means of making contact with the empiricist and naturalist outlooks of our time. He does not enable us to relate Christian affirmations to those operating on these terms. Frei in effect argues that "the provincialism of this outlook"[30] leaves us stranded at two of the points where it is most imperative that theology find a way of speaking meaningfully. The apologetic value of a theology that operates on the assumption that "reality is altogether historical" is limited particularly in the context of Moltmann's own determination to speak to the spirit of the age and the formation of its thought processes.

Moltmann, along with Pannenberg, is being criticized for his implicit confidence that the task of theology is basically to interpret for today the meaning of the Word given in Scripture. The assumption pervades the early chapters of *The Theology of Hope* that theologians and their constituencies are still secure in the viability of language about transcendence. All the Biblical message needs is the right ordering of priorities and meaningful translation in order to interact with the modern consciousness. One can and must begin with divine revelation received in faith and proceed to make it intelligible; the principal objective is communicable interpretation. It is precisely at this point that Langdon Gilkey enters a protest. He acknowledges that theologians like Moltmann, unlike their neo-orthodox predecessors, "express an orientation *outward* into the political, public world of social history, and *forward* to the future. . . . In this way, they . . . seek . . . to be both secular and Christian . . . [but] since they depend epistemologically on the Word of God in Scripture, they seem to this writer to beg as well the questions of meaning and authority in religious language."[31] Gilkey's contention, as we saw in the first chapter, is that we can no longer begin in the confidence that transcendence is accepted as a realm of meaningful discourse. Moltmann's theology is vulnerable in that it does not face the depths of the problem as it is formed in our time: the issue of whether or not it is possible to talk about God at all.

Yet for the distinctive way in which Moltmann is interpreting God as the promise of a qualitatively new future, he has impressed a new theological generation with the relevance of theology to their lived experience of anticipations and their concerns for humanizing the social order.

POSTSCRIPT

THE CURRENT THEOLOGICAL SCENE, contoured as it is by a determination to explore the reality of God, does not drive toward conclusions or lend itself to generalizations. Prevailing trends and symphonic variation on themes are conspicuous by their absence. Inevitably, theologians are asked to assess the present state of thought and project the next stage of development. There are times when this can be done with some precision. Ours is not one of them. How can one discern a trend and extrapolate when the pendulum is swinging to the right and to the left simultaneously? Some have argued that what lies ahead is a clear emphasis upon the imminence of God and the humanity of Jesus, while the transcendence of God and the divinity of Jesus will recede in importance. Certainly this is a viable forecast if one is attentive to theologians like Paul van Buren and Fritz Buri. But Wolfhart Pannenberg and Jürgen Moltmann are pressing in the opposite direction. It might be said with some justification that in the main-line Protestantism today there is no theological position for which one cannot find a contemporary counterpart. While we always have with us a range of thought, what is intriguing now is the spectrum within the center. The middle ground has been expanded drastically. When some conservatives rushed to embrace Pannenberg, he drew lines that defined his work in the mainstream and not in their camp.

Gordon Kaufman, of Harvard Divinity School, made a perceptive comment about our time when he wrote that we are all doing "experiments in thought,"[1] struggling to press through to the implications of one set of premises or another. By their very nature, experiments are conducted in an environment where there is discontent with available conceptualizations. They are an attempt to take account of the data in a more viable, valid, or meaningful way. Neither the culture nor the community of faith is supportive of any particular way of dealing with the reality of God. In this study, we have witnessed theologians grappling with the question of God with premises drawn from existentialism, process philosophy, linguistic analysis, as well as several brands of futurity. Each is indeed an "experiment in thought" and is an attempt to work through the matters of faith on its terms. No one working model has emerged that seems to best the others—except to those who advocate it!

We have pressed against each theologian in our study the question, Where in our lived experience does God become real? The assumption has been that the issues are now defined on the level of "meaning" rather than "validity." While the six theologians after Barth and Bultmann are responsive to this inquiry, some lend themselves more readily than others to this form of interrogation. Bonhoeffer calls for responsiveness to the secular world on its own terms, but does not provide us with much evidence of what it would be like to develop a secular interpretation of the gospel. Van Buren, Ogden, and Buri in quite different ways build from our lived experience to a conceptualization of what faith means in our time. Pannenberg and Moltmann appeal to lived experience, but continue to do so on the premise that the divine-human encounter is not in serious jeopardy. Their attempt to make faith plausible is still essentially deductive; it is confident of the viability of tradition authentically interpreted. By contrast, van Buren, Ogden, and Buri tend to be more inductive. They work from what Peter Berger calls "generally accessible experience"[2] to the symbolization of that in the Christian tradition. Their disposition is to sort out that in our lived experience which points beyond itself and flashes "a signal of transcendence." As such they may tend to be more persuasive in our secular culture. Some will question their faithfulness to the gospel. The issue is the degree to which one allows the lived experience to be normative. Pannenberg and Moltmann are clearly more cautious in this regard than van Buren, Ogden, and Buri.

There is no reason to believe that the vitality in the issue of God and the range of "experiments in thought" will abate in the immediate future. Diversity in approaches is supported in part by a culture that has dissolved the forces of cohesion which permitted more common ways of doing theology. But it is as well a function of the opaqueness of theology's subject which is productive of variety. The reality of God does not admit rays of light that illuminate his nature in comprehensible and definitive terms. The Godness of God is affirmed in his opaqueness.

NOTES

INTRODUCTION:
THE NEW SEARCH FOR THE MEANING OF GOD

1. Carl E. Braaten, *The Future of God* (Harper & Row, Publishers, Inc., 1969), p. 9.

2. Langdon B. Gilkey, *Naming the Whirlwind: The Renewal of God-Language* (The Bobbs-Merrill Company, Inc., 1969), pp. 12–20.

3. Martin E. Marty, *Varieties of Unbelief* (Holt, Rinehart and Winston, Inc., 1964), p. 145.

4. Kenneth Cauthen, *Science, Secularization, and God* (Abingdon Press, 1969), p. 32.

5. Gilkey, *Naming the Whirlwind: The Renewal of God-Language,* p. 63.

CHAPTER 1   KARL BARTH AND RUDOLF BULTMANN:
GOD AS REVEALED IN ENCOUNTER

1. Robert McAfee Brown, quoted in *The Christian Century,* March 26, 1969, p. 394.

2. Karl Barth, *The Humanity of God* (John Knox Press, 1960), p. 14.

3. Karl Barth, *Church Dogmatics II/2* (Edinburgh: T. & T. Clark, 1957), p. 94.

4. *Ibid.,* p. 116.

5. *Ibid.,* p. 117.

6. *Ibid.*, p. 197.

7. *Ibid.*, pp. 309–310.

8. Karl Barth, *Church Dogmatics II/1* (Edinburgh: T. & T. Clark, 1957), p. 265.

9. *Ibid.*, p. 276.

10. *Ibid.*, p. 278.

11. *Ibid.*, p. 279.

12. *Ibid.*, p. 280.

13. *Ibid.*, p. 283.

14. *Ibid.*, p. 300.

15. *Ibid.*, p. 303.

16. *Ibid.*, p. 314.

17. Barth, *The Humanity of God*, p. 46.

18. Rudolf Bultmann, *Jesus Christ and Mythology* (Charles Scribner's Sons, 1958), pp. 50–51.

19. *Ibid.*, pp. 52–53.

20. Rudolf Bultmann, *Essays, Philosophical and Theological* (The Macmillan Company, 1955), pp. 2–5.

21. *Ibid.*, p. 5.

22. *Ibid.*, p. 11.

23. Rudolf Bultmann, "New Testament and Mythology," in Hans Werner Bartsch (ed.), *Kerygma and Myth* (Harper & Brothers, Harper Torchbooks, 1954), p. 41.

24. *Ibid.*, p. 2.

25. *Ibid.*, p. 10.

26. Bultmann, *Essays, Philosophical and Theological*, p. 256.

27. Gilkey, *Naming the Whirlwind: The Renewal of God-Language*, p. 102.

CHAPTER 2 DIETRICH BONHOEFFER:
GOD AS WORLDLY AND POWERLESS

1. Eberhard Bethge, "Turning Points in Bonhoeffer's Life and Thought," *Union Seminary Quarterly Review*, Fall, 1967, p. 9.

2. Dietrich Bonhoeffer, *Prisoner for God* (The Macmillan Company, 1957), pp. 178–181.

3. *Ibid.*, p. 163.

4. *Ibid.*, p. 164.

5. Harry E. Smith, *Secularization and the University* (John Knox Press, 1968), p. 51.

6. Bonhoeffer, *Prisoner for God,* p. 125.

7. *Ibid.,* p. 122.

8. *Ibid.*

9. *Ibid.,* p. 140.

10. *Ibid.,* pp. 140–141.

11. *Ibid.,* p. 124.

12. *Ibid.,* p. 164.

13. *Ibid.,* p. 179.

14. Paul M. van Buren, "Bonhoeffer's Paradox: Living with God Without God," *Union Seminary Quarterly Review,* Fall, 1967, p. 49.

15. Bonhoeffer, *Prisoner for God,* p. 164.

16. *Ibid.,* p. 124.

17. Dietrich Bonhoeffer, *Life Together* (Harper & Brothers, 1954), p. 43.

18. *Ibid.,* p. 13.

19. Bonhoeffer, *Prisoner for God,* p. 179.

20. Dietrich Bonhoeffer, *Ethics* (The Macmillan Company, 1955), p. 64.

21. *Ibid.,* p. 65.

22. Van Buren, "Bonhoeffer's Paradox: Living with God Without God," p. 46.

23. Bonhoeffer, *Prisoner for God,* p. 126.

24. *Ibid.,* p. 149.

25. Gilkey, *Naming the Whirlwind: The Renewal of God-Language,* p. 108.

26. Schubert M. Ogden, *The Reality of God* (Harper & Row, Publishers, Inc., 1963), p. 54.

27. Paul Lehmann, "Faith and Worldliness in Bonhoeffer's Thought," *Union Seminary Quarterly Review,* Fall, 1967, pp. 32–33.

28. Dietrich Bonhoeffer, *No Rusty Swords* (William Collins Sons & Co., Ltd., 1965), pp. 309–310.

29. John D. Godsey, *The Theology of Dietrich Bonhoeffer* (The Westminster Press, 1960), p. 274.

30. Bonhoeffer, *Prisoner for God,* p. 169.

CHAPTER 3   PAUL M. VAN BUREN:
GOD AS MEANINGLESS DISCOURSE

1. Paul M. van Buren, *The Secular Meaning of the Gospel* (The Macmillan Company, 1963), p. 2.

2. Paul M. van Buren, *Theological Explorations* (The Macmillan Company, 1968), pp. 30–31.

3. Van Buren, *The Secular Meaning of the Gospel,* p. 17.

4. *Ibid.,* p. 15.

5. *Ibid.,* p. 16.

6. *Ibid.*

7. *Ibid.,* p. 105.

8. *Ibid.,* p. 84.

9. Ved Mehta, "Profiles: The New Theologians," *The New Yorker,* Nov. 13, 1965.

10. Van Buren, *The Secular Meaning of the Gospel,* p. 120.

11. *Ibid.,* pp. 121–123.

12. *Ibid.,* p. 125.

13. *Ibid.,* p. 126.

14. *Ibid.,* p. 132.

15. *Ibid.,* p. 138.

16. *Ibid.,* p. 141.

17. Langdon B. Gilkey, "A New Linguistic Madness," in Martin E. Marty and Dean G. Peerman (eds.), *New Theology No. 2* (The Macmillan Company, 1965), p. 89.

18. Van Buren, *Theological Explorations,* p. 46.

19. Thomas W. Ogletree, *The Death of God Controversy* (Abingdon Press, 1966), p. 58.

20. Gilkey, *Naming the Whirlwind: The Renewal of God-Language,* p. 236.

21. *Ibid.,* p. 238.

22. Harmon Holcomb, "Christology Without God," *Foundations,* January, 1965, p. 55.

23. *Ibid.,* p. 56.

24. Van Buren, *The Secular Meaning of the Gospel,* p. 132.

25. *Ibid.,* p. 133.

26. *Ibid.,* p. 163.

27. *Ibid.,* p. 150.

28. Gilkey, *Naming the Whirlwind: The Renewal of God-Language,* p. 153.

29. Langdon B. Gilkey, "A New Linguistic Madness," p. 49.

CHAPTER 4   SCHUBERT M. OGDEN: GOD AS PERFECT BECOMING

1. Schubert M. Ogden, *The Reality of God* (Harper & Row, Publishers, Inc. 1966) p. 14.
2. *Ibid.*
3. *Ibid.*, p. 4.
4. Schubert M. Ogden, "Toward a New Theism," in *Theology in Crisis: A Colloquium on the Credibility of God* (Muskingum College, March 20–21, 1967), p. 7.
5. *Ibid.*, p. 8.
6. *Ibid.*, p. 9.
7. Ogden, *The Reality of God,* p. 18.
8. *Ibid.*, p. 18.
9. *Ibid.*, p. 21.
10. *Ibid.*, p. 23.
11. Ogden, "Toward a New Theism," p. 12.
12. *Ibid.*, p. 34.
13. *Ibid.*, p. 35.
14. *Ibid.*, p. 37.
15. Ogden, *The Reality of God,* p. 48.
16. *Ibid.*, p. 57.
17. *Ibid.*, p. 58.
18. *Ibid.*, p. 59.
19. *Ibid.*, p. 60.
20. Ogden, "Toward a New Theism," p. 16.
21. Ogden, *The Reality of God,* p. 64.
22. Schubert M. Ogden, *Christ Without Myth* (Harper & Row, Publishers, Inc, 1961), pp. 111 ff.
23. Ogden, *The Reality of God,* pp. 90–91.
24. Ogden, *Christ Without Myth,* pp. 143–144.
25. Carl E. Braaten, *New Directions in Theology Today, Volume II: History and Hermeneutics* (The Westminster Press, 1966), pp. 85–86.
26. Cauthen, *Science, Secularization, and God,* p. 166.
27. *Ibid.*, p. 170.

28. Gilkey, *Naming the Whirlwind: The Renewal of God-Language,* p. 183.

29. Ogden, *The Reality of God,* p. 119.

30. Gilkey, *Naming the Whirlwind: The Renewal of God-Language,* p. 223.

CHAPTER 5   FRITZ BURI:
GOD AS THE UNCONDITIONEDNESS OF RESPONSIBILITY

1. Fritz Buri, *Christian Faith in Our Time* (The Macmillan Company, 1966), pp. 11–12.

2. *Ibid.,* p. 12.

3. *Ibid.,* p. 47.

4. Fritz Buri, *Theology of Existence* (The Attic Press, Inc., 1965), p. x.

5. *Ibid.,* p. 21.

6. *Ibid.,* p. 76.

7. Fritz Buri, *How Can We Still Speak Responsibly of God?* (Fortress Press, 1968), p. 1.

8. *Ibid.,* p. 2.

9. *Ibid.,* p. 15.

10. *Ibid.,* p. 16.

11. *Ibid.,* p. 18.

12. *Ibid.,* p. 19.

13. *Ibid.,* p. 20.

14. *Ibid.,* p. 22.

15. *Ibid.,* p. 23.

16. *Ibid.,* p. 26.

17. *Ibid.*

18. *Ibid.,* p. 27.

19. *Ibid.*

20. *Ibid.,* pp. 28–29.

21. *Ibid.,* p. 28.

22. *Ibid.,* p. 30.

23. *Ibid.,* p. 33.

24. *Ibid.*

25. John Macquarrie, *The Scope of Demythologizing* (London: SCM Press, Ltd., 1960), pp. 132–133.

26. *Ibid.,* p. 135.

27. *Ibid.,* p. 150.
28. *Ibid.*
29. *Ibid.,* p. 151.
30. *Ibid.,* p. 152.
31. John Macquarrie, review of *How Can We Still Speak Responsibly of God?* in *Union Seminary Quarterly Review,* Fall, 1968, p. 95.

CHAPTER 6 WOLFHART PANNENBERG:
GOD AS THE POWER OF THE FUTURE

1. Wolfhart Pannenberg, quoted in Braaten, *History and Hermeneutics,* pp. 28–29.
2. *Ibid.,* p. 29.
3. Wolfhart Pannenberg, *Jesus—God and Man,* tr. by Lewis L. Wilkins and Duane A. Priebe (The Westminster Press, 1968), pp. 19–20.
4. *Ibid.,* p. 23.
5. *Ibid.,* p. 24.
6. *Ibid.,* pp. 33–37.
7. *Ibid.,* p. 36.
8. *Ibid.,* p. 38.
9. *Ibid.,* pp. 66 ff.
10. *Ibid.,* p. 74.
11. *Ibid.,* p. 89.
12. *Ibid.*
13. *Ibid.,* p. 98.
14. Wolfhart Pannenberg, *Theology and the Kingdom of God* (The Westminster Press, 1969), p. 52.
15. *Ibid.,* p. 53.
16. *Ibid.*
17. *Ibid.,* p. 55.
18. *Ibid.*
19. *Ibid.,* p. 56.
20. *Ibid.*
21. *Ibid.,* p. 57.
22. *Ibid.*
23. *Ibid.,* p. 58.
24. *Ibid.*

25. *Ibid.*, p. 59.
26. *Ibid.*
27. *Ibid.*, p. 61.
28. *Ibid.*, p. 62.
29. *Ibid.*, p. 63.
30. *Ibid.*, p. 61.
31. Richard John Neuhaus, "Wolfhart Pannenberg: Profile of a Theologian," in *ibid.*, p. 28.
32. Helmut Gollwitzer, *The Existence of God as Confessed by Faith,* tr. by James W. Leitch (The Westminster Press, 1965), pp. 144–145.
33. Braaten, *History and Hermeneutics,* p. 50.
34. John B. Cobb, Jr., "Wolfhart Pannenberg's *Jesus—God and Man," The Journal of Religion,* April, 1969, p. 192.
35. *Ibid.*, p. 199.

CHAPTER 7   JÜRGEN MOLTMANN:
GOD AS THE PROMISE OF A NEW FUTURE

1. Jürgen Moltmann, quoted by Carl E. Braaten, "Toward a Theology of Hope," in Martin E. Marty and Dean G. Peerman (eds.), *New Theology, No. 5* (The Macmillan Company, 1968), p. 97.
2. Jürgen Moltmann, *Religion, Revolution, and the Future* (Charles Scribner's Sons, 1969), p. 149.
3. *Ibid.*, p. 152.
4. *Ibid.*, pp. 153–176.
5. Jürgen Moltmann, *The Theology of Hope* (Harper & Row, Publishers, Inc., 1967), p. 16.
6. *Ibid.*, p. 17.
7. *Ibid.*
8. *Ibid.*, p. 21.
9. Moltmann, *Religion, Revolution, and the Future,* p. 212.
10. *Ibid.*, p. 121.
11. Moltmann, *The Theology of Hope,* p. 44.
12. *Ibid.*, p. 85.
13. *Ibid.*, p. 58.
14. *Ibid.*, p. 62.
15. *Ibid.*, p. 116.

16. *Ibid.*, pp. 117–118.

17. *Ibid.*, p. 120.

18. Moltmann, *Religion, Revolution, and the Future*, p. 7.

19. *Ibid.*, p. 12.

20. *Ibid.*, p. 13.

21. *Ibid.*, p. 37.

22. *Ibid.*, p. 53.

23. *Ibid.*, p. 63.

24. *Ibid.*, p. 209.

25. *Ibid.*

26. *Ibid.*, p. 53.

27. Peter Berger, *The Rumor of Angels* (Doubleday & Company, Inc., 1969), p. 26.

28. *Ibid.*, p. 27.

29. Hans W. Frei, review of *The Theology of Hope*, in *Union Seminary Quarterly Review*, Spring, 1968, p. 272.

30. *Ibid.*, p. 271.

31. Gilkey, *Naming the Whirlwind: The Renewal of God-Language*, p. 175n.

POSTSCRIPT

1. Gordon Kaufman, "Theological Historicism as an Experiment in Thought," *The Christian Century*, March 2, 1966, p. 268.

2. Berger, *The Rumor of Angels*, p. 96.